Girls' Secondary Education in the Western World:
From the 18th to the 20th Century
Edited by James C. Albisetti, Joyce Goodman, and Rebecca Rogers
(2010)

Race-Class Relations and Integration in Secondary Education:
The Case of Miller High
By Caroline Eick
(2010)

Teaching Harry Potter:
The Power of Imagination in Multicultural Classrooms
By Catherine L. Belcher and Becky Herr Stephenson
(2011)

SECONDARY EDUCATION IN A CHANGING WORLD

Series editors: Barry M. Franklin and Gary McCulloch

Published by Palgrave Macmillan:

TEACHING HARRY POTTER

THE POWER OF IMAGINATION IN MULTICULTURAL CLASSROOMS

CATHERINE L. BELCHER

AND

BECKY HERR STEPHENSON

palgrave
macmillan

TEACHING HARRY POTTER

Copyright © Catherine L. Belcher and Becky Herr Stephenson, 2011.

All rights reserved.

First published in 2011 by
PALGRAVE MACMILLAN®
in the United States—a division of St. Martin's Press LLC,
175 Fifth Avenue, New York, NY 10010.

Where this book is distributed in the UK, Europe and the rest of the
world, this is by Palgrave Macmillan, a division of Macmillan Publishers
Limited, registered in England, company number 785998, of Houndmills,
Basingstoke, Hampshire RG21 6XS.

Palgrave Macmillan is the global academic imprint of the above companies
and has companies and representatives throughout the world.

Palgrave® and Macmillan® are registered trademarks in the United States,
the United Kingdom, Europe and other countries.

ISBN: 978–0–230–11028–1

Library of Congress Cataloging-in-Publication Data

Belcher, Catherine L., 1968–
    Teaching Harry Potter : the power of imagination in multicultural
classrooms / Catherine L. Belcher, Becky Herr Stephenson.
        p. cm.—(Secondary education in a changing world)
    Includes bibliographical references.
    ISBN-13: 978–0–230–11028–1
    ISBN-10: 0–230–11028–2
    1. Rowling, J. K.—Study and teaching—Case studies. 2. Popular
literature—Study and teaching—Case studies. 3. Multicultural
education—California—Case studies. 4. Creative teaching—Case
studies. 5. Critical pedagogy—United States. 6. Education and
state—United States. I. Herr-Stephenson, Becky. II. Title.

PR6068.O93Z535 2011
823'.914—dc22   2011000907

A catalogue record of the book is available from the British Library.

Design by Newgen Imaging Systems (P) Ltd., Chennai, India.

First edition: August 2011

10 9 8 7 6 5 4 3 2 1

Transferred to Digital Printing in 2012

To the amazing Aitana:
without you, there would be no story

Contents

Series Editors' Foreword

Among the educational issues affecting policymakers, public officials, and citizens in modern, democratic, and industrial societies, none has been more contentious than the role of secondary schooling. In developing the Secondary Education in a Changing World series with Palgrave Macmillan, our intent is to provide a venue for scholars in different national settings to explore critical and controversial issues surrounding secondary education. We envision our series as a place for the airing and resolution of these controversial issues.

More than a century has elapsed since Emile Durkheim argued the importance of studying secondary education as a unity, rather than in relation to the wide range of subjects and the division of pedagogical labor of which it was composed. Only thus, he insisted, would it be possible to have the ends and aims of secondary education constantly in view. The failure to do so accounted for a great deal of the difficulty with which secondary education was faced. First, it meant that secondary education was "intellectually disorientated," between "a past which is dying and a future which is still undecided," and as a result "lacks the vigor and vitality which it once possessed" (Durkheim 1938/1977: 8). Second, the institutions of secondary education were not understood adequately in relation to their past, which was "the soil which nourished them and gave them their present meaning, and apart from which they cannot be examined without a great deal of impoverishment and distortion" (10). And third, it was difficult for secondary school teachers, who were responsible for putting policy reforms into practice, to understand the nature of the problems and issues that prompted them.

In the early years of the twenty-first century, Durkheim's strictures still have resonance. The intellectual disorientation of secondary education is more evident than ever as it is caught up in successive waves of policy changes. The connections between the present and the past have become increasingly hard to trace and untangle. Moreover, the distance between policymakers on the one hand and the practitioners on the other has rarely seemed as immense as it is today. The key mission of the current series of books is, in the spirit of Durkheim, to address these underlying dilemmas of secondary education and to play a part in resolving them.

Teaching Harry Potter: The Power of Imagination in Multicultural Classrooms, by Catherine L. Belcher and Becky Herr Stephenson, contributes to this broad mission through the inspired readings of the world of Harry Potter in the work of three Californian schoolteachers. Andrew is a teacher of English in a charter school in Los Angeles with African-American students; Allegra is a special education teacher in an urban school in Watts; Sandra is a Latina elementary school teacher (second grade) who reads *Harry Potter* to her class in Spanish. They respond to their challenging school environments (not all of them secondary schools) by calling in their different ways on the "magic" of *Harry Potter*, a global publishing phenomenon that has already broken all sales records and transcended cultural boundaries. The authors allow these teachers to speak for themselves in voices that resonate with authenticity and integrity, and also connect their narratives in systematic fashion with the challenges of contemporary schools, popular culture, and education policy.

The dynamics of educational practice and policy are much in evidence throughout this volume. It reflects on ways of embedding technology into the everyday life of schools and on the nature of critical pedagogy and media literacy. At the same time, it shows how external pressures affect the practices of teachers as it provides a vivid commentary on contemporary education in its historical and social contexts. The image of the barrier at platform 9 and $^{3/4}$, separating the magical and Muggle worlds and yet also a bridge between them that can be challenged and subverted, is a classic device in a work that contrives both to extol magic and yet also to be fundamentally realistic about the challenges and opportunities facing teachers in the classroom.

Teaching Harry Potter is the 12th volume to be published in our series. It critiques the social and cultural dimensions of schooling, provides original insights on policy and practice, and engages with interdisciplinary methods in an exemplary and path-breaking manner. It extends the agenda of our series in novel directions. As we see the trajectory of the series advancing further during the next few years, our intent is to seek additional volumes that bring these issues still further to the attention of studies in secondary education.

BARRY M. FRANKLIN AND GARY MCCULLOCH
Series Coeditors

Acknowledgments

Our worlds have intersected thanks to The Boy-Who-Lived, and for that we are extremely thankful. We are also grateful for the assistance and support of the following people for helping us make this project possible.

First, we thank Sandra, Andrew, and Allegra, for generously sharing their inspiring stories. Your love for your students and your work stands at the heart of this book.

We also thank the numerous teachers we have met in other venues, including Nick, Dave, and Dana, who listened to our ideas with great enthusiasm and asked wonderful questions.

Without our behind-the-scenes "manager/roadie/life support," Delia Montesinos, our blog would be Tweet-less and Cathy would have lost her mind long ago. Thank you for taking the journey with us and making sure we always had chocolate.

Thanks to Andrew Slack and Karen Bernstein of the Harry Potter Alliance—Rock on!

Thanks to Edmund Kern for your words of wisdom.

We each also have colleagues, friends, and family whom we wish to acknowledge.

Catherine's Acknowledgments

I am incredibly grateful to my coauthor Becky—thank you for your Ravenclaw brilliance and your friendship. I also thank Kathleen Hall and Matthew Riggan at the University of Pennsylvania, who, when I first began to write about schools and *Harry Potter*, only had words of encouragement. Ana Serrano, Jennie Spencer Greene, and Marta Baltodano read the original proposal and provided feedback and support through the process of putting the book together. I appreciate your guidance more than you know. To my colleagues at LA's Promise, thank you for your patience and incredible enthusiasm as I worked to complete the manuscript.

I must also acknowledge my students who taught me so much about teaching and reminded me what it means to actually walk the path. Thank your for your inspiration. I hope you see something of yourselves in what is written here.

Thank you as well to my family and friends who have tolerated—and enjoyed—a life saturated with *Harry Potter* for years now. I especially want to thank my mom for reading the books and joining the fun, my husband, Jeff Fear, who believed in this project from the very outset and never wavered, and my daughter Aitana who, while a *Potter* fan herself, will be very glad to see this book in its final form so that we can get on with other things, preferably wrock concerts.

Becky's Acknowledgments

My biggest thanks goes to Cathy, for being a magical coauthor and friend. I also thank my colleagues and friends from the Digital Youth Project, especially Mimi Ito, Heather Horst, Dan Perkel, Christo Sims, and C. J. Pascoe, for encouraging me to think about the *Harry Potter* fandom as a place for learning, shaping my research approach, and indulging me in what has turned out to be four-plus years of geeking out over Harry. Thanks too to my colleagues and mentors from the University of Southern California, the University of California Humanities Research Institute, and the Joan Ganz Cooney Center at Sesame Workshop for their feedback and support during our research and writing. Finally, I thank my family, especially my parents, who helped foster my love of reading, and John, who constantly encourages me to imagine better for myself and others.

Introduction: Why Harry?

He'll be famous—a legend—I wouldn't be surprised if today was known as Harry Potter Day in the future—there will be books written about Harry— every child in our world will know his name![1]

No doubt, there is something about Harry. Whether you have read the books, seen the movies, love him or not, you know Harry Potter. The worldwide phenomenon and media franchise spurred by the young wizard has made his name an indelible part of popular culture. Following the initial printing of 12 million copies of the final book in the series, 2007's *Harry Potter and the Deathly Hallows*, 133.5 million *Harry Potter* books were in print in the United States. The first six books had sold an estimated 325 million copies worldwide.[2] In addition to the books, the *Harry Potter* franchise includes eight feature films (seven released at the time of this writing, with *Harry Potter and the Deathly Hallows* Part II scheduled for release in July 2011). The film version of *Harry Potter and the Deathly Hallows*, released in November 2010, garnered $125.2 million in its first weekend domestically and another $205 million internationally, one of the biggest global debuts to date.[3]

While *Harry Potter's* ubiquitousness is worthy of study on its own,[4] his pervasiveness is not what motivated us to pen this book. To our minds, the heart of the matter lies at the core of the phenomenon, in the fact that *Harry Potter* is a set of books that have been, and continue to be, read by children and adults all over the world. The books' compelling story of love and perseverance holds such cross-cultural appeal that they have been translated into 69 languages and distributed in more than 200 countries.[5] There is no denying it; Harry encourages people, especially kids, to read. Educators and librarians attest to Potter's effect on reluctant readers, who often find their *Harry Potter* experience to be the "hook" that helps them connect with reading.[6]

The results of a 2008 report on family reading, notably released by Scholastic, the U.S. publisher of the *Potter* series, showed that 81 percent of parents surveyed said that reading *Harry Potter* improved their child's enjoyment of reading; 74 percent of children and 79 percent of parents surveyed reported that reading *Harry Potter* led to interest in reading other books.[7] In Scholastic's 2010 report on family reading, *Harry Potter* remains a top pick for recreational reading by children and teens (ages 9–17).[8] Beyond these statistics, however, *Harry Potter* also inspires readers to create art, write their own fiction, form "Wizard Rock" (aka "Wrock") bands, create podcasts, and begin service groups in Harry's name. As educators and readers, we have found the creativity expressed during this time period incredibly exciting. It has also proven frustrating.

Simultaneous to the emergence of the *Harry Potter* phenomenon, the educational system in the United States became increasingly limiting under a growing accountability movement and the passage of the No Child Left Behind (NCLB) Act in 2000. Educational trends that could have harnessed opportunities to equalize funding and establish rich curriculum across socioeconomic lines, not to mention the potential for learning through activities such as community service projects, creative arts, and increased technology access, were either overlooked in the NCLB Act or disappeared in favor of more remediated and test-based curriculums. Since the passage of the NCLB Act in 2000, curriculum has grown particularly narrow in high-poverty and urban schools, which have had the most difficulty meeting their indicated performance indexes (as measured on examination scores) each year.

As we began the research for this book, we repeatedly heard about students motivated by their *Potter* reading experience who then found themselves facing school curriculums devoid of books. Teachers also told us about students who they thought would benefit from reading the *Potter* series in a classroom setting if only the teachers could gain access to the books, or the time needed to read them, at school. Sadly, most of the teachers with whom we spoke during our research noted that any energy around reading, creativity, new media, and civic engagement engendered by the *Potter* series has largely been squandered in public K-12 educational spaces. In this, *Harry Potter* and, increasingly, novels in general stand alongside music, art, performance, and a growing list of other such "nonessential" activities as lost educational opportunities in school.

Importantly, while opportunities to explore literacy and imagination shrink, particularly in urban schools, many students have more opportunities than ever before to engage in innovative literacy practices with media and technology in their daily lives. Despite continuing inequities in access to high-end technology and resources, including reliable high-speed Internet access, many young people rely on media such as books, television, music, video games, mobile phones, and websites to communicate with friends and others within their social networks and to develop their creative identities. Students are clearly media savvy, yet schools are either unable or choose not to utilize these skills.

In thinking on this, we decided to seek out spaces where teachers were pushing against such shortsighted limitations. Our choice to work through these critical schooling issues using the *Harry Potter* series as a reference point is deliberate and based on our assessment of the series as a powerful, cross-cultural representation of contemporary anxieties about childhood, power (both political and personal), knowledge, and education. As a school story, the series offers ample opportunities for discussion of teachers' lives and pedagogical styles, discipline, access to resources, family roles in education, political influence in schooling, and the manner in which teachers and students define themselves and their work together. Rather than write a treatise on "Why *Harry Potter* is Great for School," we believe that it makes a great deal of sense to look more closely at the actual experiences of teachers who work to use the novels and share their love of the books, as well as knowledge and appreciation of literature and literary experiences more generally, in spaces where such practice is not the norm.

Through our work, we have discovered a strong core of teachers who use *Harry Potter* in their classrooms. These teachers come from different parts of the country and from diverse school settings. They teach at all levels from elementary school to college; some are private school teachers; many teach in public schools. Despite this great diversity, we found that these teachers share important qualities: a love of *Harry Potter*, for one, but also a commitment to engendering in their students a love of story and narrative, an appreciation for reading and investigating the world around them, a sense of community around the arts, and a feeling of power that allows students to question what is put before them and to stand up to injustice. Discussions with these teachers and a desire to know what the experience of reading *Harry Potter* with a group of students looks and feels like were the impetus for the work presented here.

*   *   *

We also believe in the value of the *Potter* series, particularly given the stories that teachers have shared with us. Far from being simple children's books, the *Potter* series is rich with challenges, and the decisions that Harry constantly struggles with are not delineated in "either/or" terms; there is a great deal of gray in Harry's world. Rarely is anyone all good or all bad, and even until the end, the opportunity for redemption remains. And while Harry is the hero, he is also incredibly accessible. He is gifted, yet average. His problems, including mean teachers, school examinations, bullies, first crushes, and so on, are all common experiences, whether one is Muggle (nonmagical) or magical. Although the experience of being hunted by an evil overlord is not necessarily common among students, the challenge of having to persevere through difficult circumstances is universal and a vital lesson.

A classic characteristic of fantasy and science fiction literature is that it provides a "safe" space, a distance, if you will, that enables readers to take a critical look at modern-day problems. These opportunities abound in *Harry Potter*. Harry and his counterparts confront real-world issues such as racism, class status, war, political corruption, and ethnic cleansing, not to mention the everyday struggles of growing through childhood to adolescence and adulthood. Although not strictly a set of fantasy books, the series' parallel magical world not only comments on our own circumstances, political and ethical, but also provides amazing opportunities to discuss the nature of personal morals and choice. Historian Edmund Kern, the author of *The Wisdom of Harry Potter: What Our Favorite Hero Teaches Us About Moral Choices*, notes how Rowling addresses such challenges, stating that she presents Harry and his friends in "...ethical dilemmas requiring them to *think* in complex ways about right and wrong."[9] In progressing through the books, readers face a similar task. What does it mean to make moral choices? What does it mean to believe in equal treatment?

Harry and his friends do not shy away from such difficult questions; they accept the challenges presented to them, although they sometimes struggle in doing so. Harry, Ron, and Hermione show themselves to not simply be "heroes," but brave kids who *think* through their problems, usually in a group process. By the end of the series, their accumulated body of knowledge, garnered from school, learned folklore, long discussions with key informants (usually adults), a great deal of reading (on Hermione's part, in particular), and experience (through *doing*), allows them to finally unravel the intricate mysteries that they have faced and overcome the formidable challenges placed before them. Their path is not easy, quick, or clear, yet the kids persist, all the while thinking through the tasks at hand. What role, then, can children and young adults play in activist causes and in effecting change? What does it mean to be "brave?" The examination of such questions is particularly relevant given the difficult circumstances faced by both the teachers and the students featured here.

Approach and Organization of the Book

Teaching Harry Potter draws on established frameworks of critical pedagogy and media literacy and is heavily based in practitioner research. Although our emphasis on critical pedagogy and popular culture might seem to some a radical way of thinking about education, it is important to note that we actually advocate some very traditional ideas about school: students should learn to read; they should read with their teachers and with each other; and they should understand what they read and make sense of the vocabulary, ideas, and stories presented. Several of our key beliefs about teaching are even more traditional: teachers should be respected as professionals; they should be allowed to develop a personal pedagogical style and make choices about their teaching based on the needs of their students. This perspective drives a great deal of our approach.

One unique aspect of *Teaching Harry Potter* is the involvement of the teachers, not simply as interview subjects or observed participants, but as co-creators of the project and the text. We wanted readers to hear the teachers' voices directly. In this respect, *Teaching Harry Potter* is a shared work.

Given this, the teacher chapters are presented in narrative, rather than traditional academic form. This decision was based primarily in the teachers' own approach to our questions about their beliefs regarding their students, schools, classrooms, and practice. In working with us, they each desired to tell their own stories—and so they did. Giving the teachers voice, regardless of how methodologically "messy"[10] it might seem, served as our priority. Gloria Ladson-Billings's extensive use of "story" in her discussion of teachers' practice in *The Dreamkeepers* also proved influential here.[11] A great deal of power lies in such narratives, and we do not hear them often enough.

The book does not focus on "How to Teach *Harry Potter*," but instead explores the teachers' broader experiences as they shared the books with their students. Given the current educational climate of high-stakes testing, standardized curriculum, and "approved" reading lists, incorporating unauthorized and (in some contexts) controversial popular literature and media into the classroom becomes a political choice. The desire to understand the process and politics of *choosing* to teach *Harry Potter,* and to illuminate the resulting classroom experience, motivates our exploration of their work.

The book, then, utilizes four frameworks. First, we focus on the use of critical pedagogy that accesses prior student knowledge, including home and popular culture, builds academic skills, and establishes an environment where students and teachers engage in open, critical discourse. To our minds, *Harry Potter* provides a meeting space, much like hip-hop or popular film, to elaborate on traditional academic experiences (i.e., reading/writing/social studies). In turn, this space provides a platform from which to both access and critique material. Here we borrow from researchers Duncan-Andrade and Morrell who state "...we recognized the pedagogical potential of tapping into young people's everyday experiences as participants in popular culture to scaffold academic literacies..."[12] In essence, students use what they know to build a bridge to knowing more.

Second, we utilize critical media literacy as an approach to understanding media as a social, cultural, political, and economic system through which messages are created and circulated. This type of media education aims to teach students to deconstruct, discuss, and create media, especially encouraging production that unpacks the hegemonic messages of mainstream media and thus better represents the realities of students' own lives. Very much aligned with the goals of critical pedagogy, critical media literacy engages the cultural politics of difference, looking closely at places where media hide, highlight, and (mis)represent difference.[13]

At the same time that we recognize the power and possibilities of teaching critical media literacy through popular culture, we recognize that popular culture (including, but not limited to, *Harry Potter*) is an important part of youth culture that is separate from the culture and expectations of schools. Our third framework, new media and youth culture, brings careful attention to the ways in which structures of power in schools encourage, limit, or change the way students understand the *Harry Potter* series as part of their own popular culture. As readers and media users, the teachers and students involved in this project have many different relationships with the *Potter* books and related media; few, if any, of these relationships should be described in terms of passive consumption, as reading is always a process of negotiation between the reader and the text.[14] Indeed, the ways in which readers in this project consume texts—books, films, digital media, and so on—is highly illustrative of subversive forms of consumption, reflecting notions about youth culture, prominent in cultural theory since the 1960s, which identifies youth culture as a highly productive space for resistant readings and uses of media and consumer goods.[15]

The fourth framework, practitioner research, which looks to "represent teachers' work from teachers' own perspectives,"[16] grounds our view of teachers as collaborators on this project and informs our approach to the teachers' writing process. In addition, our collaborative approach to working with the teachers is influenced by Cochran-Smith and Lytle's "core premises," which posit that "... practitioners are deliberative intellectuals who constantly theorize practice as part of practice itself..."[17] We believe in the intellectual power of skilled teachers and firmly establish ourselves as colleagues *with*, rather than researchers *of*, the teachers featured here.

Participants

Sandra, Andrew, and Allegra, the three teachers highlighted in this book, work in challenging educational settings with children who are often marginalized by society and schools. These students and teachers are the most pressured through federal and state testing mandates. Often, their classrooms lack access to media and technology, even the books themselves. Unfortunately, as previously stated, America's urban and/or high-poverty schools increasingly see their access to literature shrinking only to be replaced by scripted curricula that provide few opportunities for variation or creative thought for both students and teachers. The teachers profiled in *Teaching Harry Potter*, however, repeatedly demonstrate that imagination is both necessary and possible—even in the most dire of educational and social circumstances. The teachers here have graciously shared their struggles and described their efforts to move beyond the constraints presented to them. Despite varying years of practice, the *Teaching Harry Potter* teachers are experts; they are the Remus Lupins and Albus Dumbledores of the nonmagical world—smart, dedicated, caring, daring, and creative professionals.

We came to know the participating teachers through our university positions; they were our students or our research site contacts, and through these relationships we came to know about the unique things that they accomplished in their classrooms. All are teachers of record, with varying approaches to educational practice, but a shared belief in the power of authentic, critical educational experiences. All of them teach in high-poverty schools in California—one in a rural, Latino community, two in urban Los Angeles. Each teacher also represents a different school age group, elementary, junior high, and high school; two are public school teachers and one taught in a charter school during our work together. Participating teachers each took part in the following:

- Regular planning conferences with the researchers over a minimum of two academic years
- Reflective practitioner research through journaling and ongoing interviews/discussions with the researchers and the other *Teaching Harry Potter* teachers
- Writing and coediting as well as final approval of their respective teacher chapters

Through ongoing dialogue about teaching practice and philosophy, the researchers and the teachers decided on a writing format (journal, extended interview) as well as the instructional focus that each practitioner would utilize. All three teachers discuss their rationale and objectives for using *Harry Potter* in their classrooms, and reflect on the classroom events that then took place as they shared the books and related media with their students.

Again, it is our goal that through their respective narratives, which are set apart in the text, the teachers' authentic voices are brought to the forefront. In our accompanying commentary, we remark and build on each teacher narrative with the goal of both drawing attention to the unique issues presented by each teacher and working to link their chapters with the larger themes presented throughout the book. In addition to Sandra, Andrew, and Allegra, readers will find three additional "Another Take" stories from Nick, Dave, and Dana describing their experiences teaching *Harry Potter* in three additional schools in California. While they are not case study teachers, they serve as representatives of the many other teachers who shared their stories with us over the course of our research.

* * *

Teaching Harry Potter also attempts to open the door connecting literature, imagination, learning, and advocacy. To that end, we explore what it means to encourage "real-world" learning through immersive educational experiences and student/community activism. Our focus in this discussion is on the work of the Harry Potter Alliance (HPA), an international nonprofit organization built upon the social justice themes of the *Potter* series. Through its activist campaigns, the HPA,[18] which includes national and international community and school-based chapters that often communicate through online media (podcasts, Twitter, online meetings), demonstrates what Rowling meant when she said "we do not need magic to change the world."[19] Rowling herself has specifically recognized the group stating, "I am honoured and humbled that Harry's name has been given to such an extraordinary campaign which really does exemplify the values for which Dumbeldore's Army fought in the books."[20]

Alliance campaigns have included efforts to raise awareness of the crisis in Darfur and to gather signatures on petitions of protest; the "Wizard Rock the Vote" campaign, which registered several hundred new voters during the 2008 presidential election; a book drive that collected more than 13,000 books, one third of which were donated to youth centers in Rwanda; and the spearheading of a drive for Haiti earthquake relief that raised $123,000 and, in partnership with Partners in Health, allowed for five cargo planes of relief supplies to be sent to the country.[21] The HPA's organic blend of popular culture, inclusive media, learning, and youth activism can be understood as an instantiation of the call to community action inherent in critical pedagogy. Our discussion of these issues with the young people active in the HPA serves as a fitting close to the work and a tangible example of the power that we all have to "imagine better."[22]

In order to build our discussion over the course of the book, those chapters that discuss and reflect on school structures, culture, and popular culture and policy—1, 3, and 5—are interspersed with the teacher narrative chapters—2, 4, and 6. In this manner, a practitioner's light is shed on the issues at hand as one moves through the book. The chapters thus build upon each other, growing a broad portrait of education policy, contemporary teaching experiences, critical media literacy, and thoughts around *Harry Potter* and its role in educational spaces. Although the book centers on how the teachers use the *Harry Potter* novels in their classrooms, the reader can likely "get the gist" of the discussion here without having read the *Potter* books, although nuances of meaning will certainly be lost. We do not provide plot synopses or character descriptions, given that these are readily available online through the myriad of fan sites that center around the books and movies, as well as J. K. Rowling's own official site. Of course, we also recommend simply reading the books. They are quite wonderful.

Chapter 1 of *Teaching Harry Potter* reflects on twenty-first-century teaching, and how the *Teaching Harry Potter* teachers push against the current deskilling and "technicizing" of the teaching profession.[23] Against the backdrop of the NCLB Act and the accountability movement, advocating for critical, culturally relevant pedagogy and the use of popular texts in the classroom may seem futile. We disagree, and argue for a view of education that looks upon teachers as creative, empowered, and intelligent decision-makers. We also look at the commonalities between the three *Teaching Harry Potter* teachers in order to gain a clearer understanding of what current educators both hold as their goals and desire in terms of the "evolution" of their profession.

While there are common threads through each, the individual teacher chapters capture a different aspect of the current educational environment, highlighting differing conflicts or tensions within the system. Chapter 2 is coauthored by Sandra, a Latina elementary school teacher in a California border town school district. She chooses to challenge her primarily Mexican American, Spanish-dominant students to read beyond the books assigned to their grade and perceived skill level. Her narrative recounts her experience of reading *Harry Potter and the Sorcerer's Stone* to her class in Spanish. For those specifically seeking to improve the educational lives of Latinos and Latino immigrant children, the bridge established through access to the students' native language resonates in a particularly significant manner.

Chapter 3 locates this book within a broader discussion of public schooling, the backdrop of current educational policy, particularly the NCLB Act, and the pressures these bring to bear on students and teachers. We also discuss the role of critical pedagogy and popular culture in education and how the *Harry Potter* novels can play a role in elaborating on established learning goals.

Chapter 4 explores how Andrew, an English teacher in a Los Angeles charter high school, utilizes the *Harry Potter* collection to contribute to urban African American students' abilities to make text-to-self and text-to-world connections when the books are viewed as literature from outside their cultural point of reference. Andrew chronicles how he challenges his students' notions of *Harry Potter* as being for "white kids." By innovatively utilizing multiple media forms, he demonstrates the accessibility of the *Potter* novels to his students who then use them to explore complex literary ideas present in the English Advanced Placement exam, and to challenge notions of what constitutes a book that is "truly literary."

Chapter 5 explores the realities and possibilities of using popular culture, digital media, and technology to support learning in and outside of schools. Highlighting the importance of thoughtful, embedded, and empowering approaches to technology, the chapter calls for innovative approaches to bridging longstanding gaps in access and participation. Drawing from each of the *Teaching Harry Potter* teachers' stories, the chapter uncovers examples of how teachers leveraged media and technology in their different schools to challenge the "legitimated" curriculum, to encourage creativity and critical thinking, and to bring out each student's magic.

Chapter 6 follows Allegra, a special education teacher at an urban middle school in Watts, California, as her class challenges labels and notions of "difference." She uses *Harry Potter and the Sorcerer's Stone* as a vehicle to discuss and think critically about what it means to be labeled as different and to explore both the benefits and the challenges of such perceptions. In teaching English/Language Arts, including a course for developing readers centered on critical reading strategies and literacy skills, Allegra encourages her students to view books (generally) as a means for learning about common life experiences. Given that her students are labeled as "special education" students, she utilizes *Sorcerer's Stone* to challenge such labels, promoting strategies that encourage her class to question the author and also make critical connections with the text.

Chapter 7 considers what happens when we are finished reading. The cases presented in this book provide rich examples of contemporary critical pedagogy and student-centered, creative, and joyous teaching; how do we translate what goes on in these classrooms to larger educational policy? How can "education" (institution-based learning) be blended with advocacy and civic participation? Using the example of the HPA, we consider the possibilities for engagement and social change presented by expanding our definitions of "education" and "learning" beyond school walls to include new parameters of learning, service, and community activism. We also then consider some of the larger education questions posed throughout.

In an age of standardized testing, test preparation and the threat of punishments for teachers and students who do not improve scores have numbed many teachers and their students to the joy of active engagement with learning and creative thought. The *Potter* novels and other such accessible literature, through their incredible acceptance by children, allow a space for that joy to reemerge. In addition, *Harry Potter* provides a literary experience that opens avenues to more. Rowling's approachable and enjoyable use of mythology and classics invites students to pursue other works that have proven influential and/or relate to Harry's world, among these history, mythology, and science.[24] Harry's struggles also invite readers to think in critical and imaginative ways about everyday experience and the world around them.

Much like Harry Potter himself, whose subversive actions throughout the series invited conflict with certain school staff and government officials, the teachers involved in this project have challenged curricular restrictions that in today's high-stakes testing environment limit their choices in severe ways. Most often, their risk-taking has paid off, resulting in incredibly moving, and instructive, teachable moments. What these teachers accomplish though the books, coupled with what they struggle to accomplish on a daily basis, requires a particular brand of, shall we say, magic.

As Dumbledore stated at the end of the movie version of *Goblet of Fire*, "Dark and difficult times lie ahead, soon we must all face the choice between what is right and what is easy."[25] For too long, educational policy has chosen the easy, quick fix, to the great detriment of many learners. It is our hope that this book will inspire thinking, dialogue about the state of teaching and education, and the identification of opportunities for educators to reclaim educational spaces for those who matter most—students.

Chapter 1

Defending the (Not Really) Dark Arts: Teaching to Break the DADA Curse*

"Did you see me take that banshee"? shouted Seamus.
"And the hand!" said Dean, waving his own around.
"And Snape in that hat!"
"And my mummy!"...
"That was the best Defense Against the Dark Arts lesson we've ever had, wasn't it?" said Ron excitedly...
"He [Lupin] seems like a very good teacher," said Hermione approvingly.[1]

"In the United States, teachers are the most inequitably distributed school resource."[2]

We have all felt the energy and excitement that Seamus, Dean, and Ron exhibit after their great Defense Against the Dark Arts (DADA) class: the feeling that we gained a new skill, learned something important that we did not know before, grew our self-confidence, and had a great time. In short, we have all experienced at least one great, successful teacher and/or teaching moment. These are events that make a significant difference in how we perceive ourselves as learners. In *Teaching Harry Potter*, these teaching events also frame how we view the value of talented teachers and everyday, extraordinary teaching.

---

* Defense Against the Dark Arts: "That job's jinxed. No one's lasted more than a year..."[3]

Unfortunately, as alluded to in Linda Darling-Hammond's quote above, highly skilled teachers, the primary catalysts for effective teaching moments, work in larger numbers in America's suburbs than in its urban and/or high-poverty neighborhoods.

Much has been written about the current state of the teaching profession in the United States, which is under great pressure to conform to mandates around testing and curriculum. As we pen this book, discussions regarding the role of teacher unions, merit pay, seniority, credentialing, and linking teacher pay to gains on student test scores swirl through the news. The latter issue has garnered particular attention given the Obama administration's current Race to the Top initiative, which, through a competitive application process, funds state reforms specifically linked to the development and scale up of standards, assessments, and data collection.[4]

Race to the Top is only the most recent policy push affecting educators. The fact that the primary teaching evaluation measure being discussed is student standardized examination scores certainly evidences what educator and philosopher Henry Giroux terms the growing "technization" of teaching. From this perspective, teachers work more as trainers, drilling a set of examination-taking techniques and giving remedial instruction, rather than serving as educators who guide students through developing critical thinking and decision-making skills.[5] Much as students' educational experiences have been stunted through such efforts, teachers' ownership over their profession has deteriorated, largely because of a dearth of authentic benchmarks for excellence in teaching. If evidence of a teacher's ability is defined primarily by his or her students' test scores, it seems unrealistic to expect teachers to be motivated to craft creative lesson plans or to risk innovation in using new resources and tools in the classroom.

Such tensions have grown out of district and school efforts to cope with the No Child Left Behind (NCLB) Act's demands for rising scores on high-stakes tests. Whereas once we sought teachers who hold expertise in subject areas and in how to work with children, schools now look for teachers who can raise test scores, and in many high-poverty areas this requires teachers to accurately follow a prescribed curriculum. Testing pressures overwhelm the idea that teachers hold a particular expertise to contribute to the profession. The belief that practitioners draw on such expertise daily to contribute to student success and the betterment of their unique school communities is also rapidly disappearing from our consciousness. Teacher researchers Cochran-Smith and Lytle note that:

> The accountability emphasis is reflected in the recurring language of outcomes, results, effectiveness, evidence, monitoring systems, test scores, adequate yearly progress, and bottom lines. Words like these have been used so consistently in everyday discourse and at every level of schooling that they are now fully normalized and neutralized ... From this perspective, it is assumed that teaching is the demonstration of that knowledge in high-stakes contexts, and differences in local settings and capacities are unimportant.[6]

Our view of teachers and their roles in classrooms and schools consciously pushes back against such limited expectations. Every day, teachers work in varied educational spaces, many of them fighting difficult, uphill battles (in many ways similar to our young wizard tasked with saving the world), and many of them working in challenging, economically strapped communities. In choosing to focus on teachers' experiences with reading books and utilizing other media forms, we present a counternarrative to those stories of teachers as failures of America's youth and instead detail spaces where we see hope for creative, innovative, dare we say—magical—teaching.

The idea that a set of popular books can offer solutions and/or commentary on current school policy may sound simplistic, but we posit that critically exploring such popular representations of education is more important than one might think. For example, beyond our critical reading of the series, this book demonstrates the impact that popular media—skillfully taught—can have in classrooms. As we shall discuss here, an educator's reading of the *Harry Potter* novels also brings to light the fact that we, the readers, know what effective, caring teaching looks like, and in Harry, we see that it can be learned and nurtured through mentorship, engagement, and experience. This is not a new idea—but it is one that educational discourse and current policy mandates regarding teaching continually fail to recognize as vital.

Instead, current policies focus on standardizing teachers' lesson delivery as well as their students' results. If the goal is to nurture and retain high-quality teachers, then these policies are seriously flawed. Threatening teachers with their jobs if they do not raise their students' test scores is simply not going to make them better teachers. It might make them more determined test tutors or drive them away from the profession altogether, but it will not make them better educators. In the same vein, a constant focus on testing certainly will not help students become more proficient at the decision-making or problem-solving skills clearly required to live successful lives.

Each of the three *Teaching Harry Potter* teachers reflects current pressures to various degrees. How they cope, push back, and/or adjust to various demands frames a great deal of their narratives. One wonders, however, given the professional climate, whether they would still be teaching were we to look in on them in five years. Certainly, the revolving door of teachers and issues with teacher quality and retention, particularly in high-poverty districts, evidence such pressures and indicate that, sadly, we might not see our teachers were we to open that future classroom door.

Defending Teaching

Much like Harry who faces a new DADA teacher every year, many students today face a revolving door of teachers, often within a single school year. High-poverty schools in urban centers often find it especially difficult to retain teachers, sometimes utilizing multiple substitutes in place of a full-time teacher for a complete school year. Therefore, while Harry's "teacher-go-round" is based in a curse, today's public school students find their loss based in a long list of systemic and culturally based pressures including layoffs (due to shrinking budgets), inadequate teacher preparation, burnout, or the lure of more lucrative prospects.[7] The frustrations of highly skilled teachers within prescriptive work environments are understandable; teaching has simply become more constrained and, for many, more professionally unfulfilling.

Arguably, public school teachers in the United States have never really enjoyed a high degree of esteem. As a profession, it does not carry the same social and economic weight as law or medicine, for example. Teachers in the United States certainly do not hold the status that teachers in many other countries have, where teaching is considered a revered or high-status position. Finland, where becoming a teacher is highly competitive, for example, benefits from a highly skilled teaching force. Darling-Hammond describes how only 15 percent of applicants to Finnish teacher education programs are accepted. Those who are then receive full funding to attend a three-year graduate-level teacher preparation program. They are also paid a living stipend.[8] It is hard to imagine such a thing occurring in the United States.

The recruitment and retention of excellent teachers remains one of the biggest challenges to improving education in the United States, yet we do very little to ensure the forms of mentorship and professional growth that have been proven to identify and retain excellent practitioners. Given the fact that teacher quality correlates highly with student success, such inaction is clearly self-defeating. In the same line of thinking, any teacher who wants to "advance" must leave the classroom to do so. Again, Darling-Hammond states, "The message is clear: Those who work with children have the lowest status; those who do not have the highest."[9] To this, we would add that those who work with high-poverty children of color hold an even lower status as evidenced in teacher salary differentials and unequal resources between suburban and high-poverty schools.[10]

One of the goals of our work with the *Teaching Harry Potter* teachers lies in defending teachers—their reputations, their voice, and their capacity for innovation and brilliance. We realize that much as doctors and lawyers, not all teachers are equally skilled. However, too often we hear the negative stories without hearing the good, likely one of the reasons we as a society have come to place so little trust in teachers' capacity to actually instruct a given curriculum. Otherwise, we would not accept lessons that are scripted down to the minute. It is also important to show what expertise and potential does lie in the profession, or again, we will neither attract new teachers nor retain the skilled pedagogues currently working in schools.

Teaching and Learning Like Heroes

From a cultural perspective, as a society we definitely share some core, common beliefs about teachers and their work. Much of these derive from our own school experiences and various media representations we accumulate from childhood. In looking directly at *Harry Potter* as an example of a school story, given our common social and media experiences, we expect that readers will recognize not only the schooling process but several teacher archetypes as well: McGonagall (stern and confident), Snape (bitter and cruel), and Lupin (caring expert) among them. Unfortunately, Rowling does not elaborate a great deal on the teachers' lives, given that we see them through Harry's eyes. Dumbledore and Snape are the only two whose backgrounds we eventually come to know, and that does not happen until the final book, *Deathly Hallows*. For this reason, nuances of the teachers' personalities and motivations are largely absent or simply alluded to, and many of the archetypes then play to stereotypes as a result. Professor Binns, for example, the history teacher who drones on unaware with little interest in the students' learning or lives, is a classic example of the "boring history teacher."

Regardless, in the Hogwarts faculty, we readers are definitely expected to *recognize* who is a good teacher and who is not. Most, if not all, of us would not choose to take Professor Binns' class, for example, which says a great deal about "us" and cross-cultural educational experiences. While we may not all agree on the specifics of how to measure certain teacher qualities such as "expertise," or which qualities to actually measure in the first place, "caring" for example, and while we will not likely all agree on who is the absolute best teacher at Hogwarts, we undoubtedly share core beliefs about which teachers should be placed on the "best of" list and could conceivably have a rather lively and productive debate about our choices.

Among the Hogwarts faculty, Remus Lupin is considered both skilled and caring.[11] His pedagogical skill also has long-term effects that resonate through to the end of the series. Lupin is the first of Harry's DADA teachers to engage the students in practical, experiential lessons, which Lupin also uses to build the students' confidence. In one particularly telling moment in *Prisoner of Azkaban*, Snape warns Lupin "not to entrust him [Neville] with anything difficult" to which Lupin counters, "I was hoping that Neville would assist me with the first stage of the operation...and I'm sure he will perform it admirably."[12] Neville's lack of confidence and difficulty with magic are common knowledge among his classmates and teachers. Lupin's choice to focus on supporting Neville is purposeful and deliberate and shows a great deal of intuitive caring.

It is Lupin who also agrees to tutor Harry outside of class in order to help him fend off the Dementors that affect him so terribly. Through these lessons, Harry learns advanced magic that serves as a direct precursor to his leadership of the student group that comes to be known as "Dumbledore's Army" or the DA. Harry's ability to produce a corporeal *Patronus* (complete a highly advanced defensive spell), learned through his tutoring with Professor Lupin, becomes a skill that not only saves Harry's life but also later convinces the other students that he is strong enough—and experienced enough—to teach them, as we shall soon recount.

Dumbledore also deserves a mention here, although the secrets that he keeps from Harry likely disqualify him for the "best of" list in many readers' eyes. While not one of Harry's official teachers, he serves as his mentor and protector. Dumbledore is also a source of extensive knowledge about magic and the Wizarding world; he was approached regarding the position as Minister of Magic (equivalent to a Prime Minister) more than once, but declined, remaining as Headmaster at Hogwarts. His decision to remain at the school, while partially a result of his wish to avoid the pitfalls of holding political power, is also commendable and instructive: highly skilled individuals (educators) who choose to remain in educational settings can make a significant, long-lasting impact on the students, teachers, and the institution.

Much as with the "best of" list, we would likely also agree on the list of Hogwarts' "worst" teachers. Glideroy Lockhart, Harry's second DADA teacher, is an obvious choice as he represents the inept charlatan who actually knows nothing about the subject that he is assigned to teach. Unfortunately, we have all likely experienced someone similar in the classroom at least once. While Lockhart's memory loss at the end of the book is not something to be wished on anyone, it certainly represents a form of payback for what he attempts to foist on his students, particularly Harry and Ron, whose memories he tries to erase lest they give away the secret of his incompetence.

Much more damaging, and likely the most often noted in this category, is Professor Umbridge, who embodies oppression and suppression in the classroom. She also represents political intrusion into educational spaces. Umbridge's brief tenure as "Hogwarts High Inquisitor" and then Headmaster (in *Order of the Phoenix*) frames Rowling's commentary on current education and social policy. Umbridge embodies state mandates at their most invasive, severe, and shortsighted. She is the politician who thinks that she knows better than the actual educators. Political gain garnered through "ordering" of the school is her priority. She arbitrarily makes and enforces mandates—"Decrees"—without considering the character and needs of the students. As a Ministry plant, her motivation derives from the fear that students will learn how to utilize defensive spells so well that they will overturn the ministry in collusion with Dumbledore. Here, Umbridge represents the worst form of corrupt paranoia as it distracts everyone from the true threat, Voldemort, who the Ministry and Umbridge refuse to acknowledge has returned.

Sadly, such forms of control have been acted out repeatedly in history, through legislation and practice that served to limit access to information or educational opportunity by race, class, gender, socioeconomic status, or political inclination. Knowledge is power, and those in control know it. If this were not the case, schools would never serve as sites of conflict. *Brown vs. Board of Education*, for example, and the resulting desegregation process in Little Rock, Arkansas, would not have ignited conflict so intense that the National Guard had to be called in to keep order. More recently, arguments over the content of history textbooks and social studies curriculum in Texas illuminate how contested school curriculum remains. Should Thomas Jefferson's role in the founding of the United States be diminished because he presented a secular viewpoint? Editing out Jefferson's participation does not change history; it only changes what is presented as truth. We still argue over whose stories to tell because the effects of those stories are powerful.

Schools have historically reflected the political climate, again, often to the detriment of students' needs, as is the case with the current use of standardized testing as the primary measure of learning and "effective" teaching. Such uniform measures are quick to employ and the results easy to compile through technology. The resulting data sets serve to provide fodder for politicians and those looking to lay the blame for low-performing schools on teachers and students. As historian Diane Ravitch states, "What matters most is for the school, the district, and the state to be able to say that more students have reached 'proficiency' "[13] on state-approved and mandated tests. Dolores Umbridge would certainly be pleased.

Rowling, in her creation of Umbridge, brings her commentary on such policies front and center. Umbridge restricts the curriculum to a ministry-approved textbook and forbids students from actually practicing the protective spells they read about. Fortunately, the students themselves cut Umbridge's term short, and they begin by enacting their own beliefs about "good teaching" and "good teachers." The DA represents Rowling's counter to Umbridge and the Ministry's oppressive control. The DA is a student group, initiated by Hermione, who convinces Harry to serve as the teacher and leader. Hermione tells the assembled group, "...well, I thought it would be good if we, well, took matters into our own hands...And by that I mean learning how to defend ourselves properly, not just theory but the real spells—."[14] In forming the DA, the students demonstrate their understanding of the value of hands-on, experiential, inclusive, and caring classroom experiences. They recognize that in Umbridge's classroom they are not receiving a good education, that the delivery of the curriculum is limited and ineffective. As Helfenbein states in his excellent essay "Conjuring Curriculum, Conjuring Control," "Harry's secret class...is a clear example of students taking charge of their own learning. Students in this case not only resist Ministry control of their curriculum but also involve themselves directly in evaluating good teaching."[15] The DA students do not just want better lessons, they want a better teacher, and this means someone who will work with them to actually practice—*do*—spell work.

In the initial conversation between Harry, Ron, and Hermione regarding formation of the DA, Harry assumes the natural choice for this "proper" teacher to be Professor Lupin. Hermione corrects him, telling Harry that she means him, and goes on to explain why Harry is her choice, "But I'm not talking about test results, Harry. Look what you've *done!*"[16] His experience and ability to share are what Hermione values. Once the group actually meets, Harry's lessons mirror those between himself and Lupin in *Prisoner of Azkaban*; they are hands-on, based in an open dialogue about what is being taught and learned. In his leadership role, Harry reflects Lupin's teaching style in his level of expertise and his willingness to consider the needs of his students and share lessons experientially. These are clearly practices that the group comes to expect from a "good teacher." Harry's favorite DADA teacher certainly left a lasting impression. Students organizing to further their own learning represents one of the primary goals of a critical, authentic approach to education; students should learn to grow to care for and represent *themselves*. In making their own decisions, they drive their own learning, and in this they complete the ultimate assessment, thinking critically and drawing on their own agency.

Readers are meant to identify with the DA; *we* are Dumbledore's Army, which means that we are expected to want to join in the experience, and not just for the Wizarding fantasy. It is supposed to be a learning experience recognized by readers as valid and important; we are supposed to view the students' work together as engaging and valuable and feel that it will help us. We are meant to desire the experience and to know its worth. Given the popularity of the novels and Harry's "heroic" place in popular culture, it is safe to say that this understanding has been reached many times over. Why then can we not see how such engagement could prove valuable in our own schools and then act on that understanding? In Chapter 7, we discuss how fans of the series have organized highly successful summer camps and advocacy groups in the spirit of learning like the DA. Why not bring the same energy to public schools?

Moving Beyond "Highly Qualified:" The *Teaching Harry Potter* Teachers

Relying on their intuition, emotion and imagination is a key ingredient in the workings of teachers who desire to create teachable moments.[17]

So, then, given the current political and educational climate, what distinguishes the *Teaching Harry Potter* teachers and what can we learn from them? To begin, the *Teaching Harry Potter* teachers teach us a great deal about resiliency and perseverance. It is important to note, though, that they are not perfect and should not be viewed in that manner. Ladson-Billings's warning about developing a "cult-of-personality" explanation for effective teaching is well made.[18] To do so runs the risk of making excellent teaching unique to a person, and not a profession. In Harry's world, for example, it would mean that there could never be another great leader for the DA, that no one else could learn from Lupin and Harry's examples to then pass on these skills. Beliefs such as these also leave little encouragement for struggling teachers who could potentially grow to become successful were the right support systems, including "high-quality professional development, peer mentoring, and classroom assignments that effectively match their training and preparation," put in place.[19]

Therefore, while we do believe the teachers here share particular qualities, it is important to note that these characteristics are rooted in the teachers' *beliefs* about their practice, the manner in which they engage these beliefs in their classroom, and how they handle the aftereffects, regardless of where these fall on the "success" spectrum. It is their reflective thought processes and the resulting choices that distinguish their teaching practice. Two pedagogical philosophies are central to their practice: critical pedagogy and culturally relevant teaching. Educator Paolo Freire's critical pedagogy advocates a "reading the world" approach to education[20] that pairs our core ideal of agency—or choice—for teachers and learners with that of reflection on the process. Through critical, reflective practice, students and teachers forge and foster reciprocal relationships; teachers are also students of the classroom experience, and students are teachers who have ideas to bring to the table and share. Critical praxis lies at the core of this, where students and teachers choose to engage a particular problem, work—research—to solve it, and reflect on the experience to then begin the cycle anew.[21] It is this process of questioning—the reflective cycle—that transforms students and teachers alike as they work together and make both content and learning their own.

Carefully enacted, a critical approach to teaching creates a community of learners, which then engages material such as *Harry Potter* in various ways: for example, understanding story; building expertise in reading, writing, and comprehension; sharing literary experiences; and drawing inferences from Harry's story and applying them to one's own journey of self-discovery. The experience of reading a book is thus complex, multifaceted, community oriented, and personal. One of the ultimate goals in developing such forms of literacy is empowerment and the growth of social consciousness. As Giroux states, the curriculum "... should be rooted in the best that has been produced by human beings and designed to both stir the imagination and empower young people with a sense of integrity, justice and hope for the future."[22]

In addition to utilizing a critical approach to education, the teachers frame the curriculum in ways that make it *culturally relevant* for their students. Coined by educator and researcher Gloria Ladson-Billings, culturally relevant teachers "see their teaching as an art rather than as a technical skill."[23] Their pedagogy is marked by a critical approach to the curriculum and equitable, connected relationships with their students. They look to build on the students' strengths and prior knowledge. Student identity, as a member of a family, a community, school, and classroom, for example, is taken into consideration and used to shape both the curriculum and learning. In this respect, the curriculum is both contestable and fluid. Such teachers work much like coaches who "... rather than expecting students to demonstrate prior knowledge and skills, [they] help students develop that knowledge by building bridges and scaffolding for learning."[24]

While they did not always necessarily intend to practice critical, culturally relevant pedagogy, *per se*, the case study teachers' belief in student agency and choice and their drive to give voice to their students and acknowledge their particular home and life experiences (funds of knowledge)[25] result in the ongoing reflective practice—praxis—that marks a critical and caring approach to education. Again, we did not ask the teachers to become critical pedagogues, although they identify themselves as such. Instead, we approached their work by utilizing a critical lens, recognizing the praxis already in place and reflecting with them about what *they* believe critical, culturally relevant pedagogy means and what they look to accomplish by incorporating these into their teaching practice.

In Chapter 2, the first *Teaching Harry Potter* teacher, Sandra, describes her decision to read *Sorcerer's Stone* in Spanish with her second graders. The moment is significant as it clearly illustrates the positive effects of joint decision making and access to curricular choices in the classroom. Sandra noted her students' growing interest in the *Harry Potter* films and books and used that enthusiasm to build an inclusive curriculum and a communal reading experience around the first *Harry Potter* book. Because her students were Spanish-language dominant, she chose to read the book in Spanish in order to make the activity more accessible and engaging for them. She then used the experience to scaffold their learning about story components and vocabulary and to build their confidence around their ability to contribute to a class discussion. If Sandra had been unwilling to engage the students' interests or refused to read to them in Spanish, imagine all that would have been lost, especially where student ownership of their learning is concerned. Sandra has been unable to replicate this experience fully since California's 1998 enactment of Proposition 227, a law prohibiting the use of native language in the classroom beyond a non-English speaking student's first year of schooling. The 12 years' worth of missed opportunities in her classroom due to this legislation are irreplaceable.

In Chapter 4, Andrew's insistence that the *Potter* books are both appropriate and accessible for his African American charter high-school students brings a clear critique of narrow curriculum and an argument for opening the door to innovation. He openly challenges assumptions voiced by both students and school staff regarding what is appropriate and accessible for his students. He is skeptical of popular opinion in his school about what his students can "handle," and, as a result, embarks on an exploratory, challenging, journey with his Advanced Placement English class. Andrew also facilitates copious opportunities for students to engage with a wide range of popular media—from books such as *Harry Potter* to popular music, films, and television. He views and utilizes popular culture as a bridge to the canonical literature students need to experience and understand for their college preparation and future success in higher education and beyond. Once learned, these new media literacy skills prove highly useful and transferable to the media students encounter in and outside of school.

Like Andrew, Allegra regularly challenges assumptions about her students' abilities through her pedagogical approach and educational philosophies. In Chapter 6, we see how she both acknowledges and moves past notions of difference placed upon her students. As a special education teacher, she is especially attuned to the importance of holding high expectations for student participation and performance. Special education students are all too often written off as problems or lost causes; without a creative and demanding teacher such as Allegra, they are practically doomed to disengagement and school failure. Allegra's dedication to challenging and inventive pedagogy that connects to students' interests and skills led her to a unique way of reading *Harry Potter* with her students, seventh graders who had basic reading skills, but who were struggling with reading fluency. Instead of requiring students to endure endless decoding drills or memorize decontextualized vocabulary words, Allegra introduced her students to the *Harry Potter* audio books, designing a read-along activity that was useful for maintaining student interest and motivation for the project while providing students with a powerful, engaging model of fluent reading.

Each *Teaching Harry Potter* teacher works in a different school context, but their philosophies—beliefs—about education and their effectiveness as pedagogues link them to one another. When we examine the teachers' narratives, the following shared commonalities emerge:

• Each desires the autonomy and planning time to make informed curricular choices. They have no trouble using a set of appropriate standards; what they want is more decision-making power about how to best meet the standards with their particular student communities. When these teachers are given the opportunity to mold the curriculum, their students respond favorably, actively participating and asking for more opportunities to do so.

• Each succeeds with students of color who traditionally do not do well in U.S. schools. These success measures include both teacher-derived and standardized testing indicators and positive feedback from school administrators and the community. This quality of teaching is directly influenced by the next point.

• Each knows the students well and exhibits a particular quality of engagement with them based in caring, high expectations, and Ladson-Billings's culturally relevant teaching. In this, each teacher utilizes the reality of the students' lives, including their interests and family/community background, to drive or enhance the curriculum.

• As critical pedagogues, each also creates a reflective, communal learning experience in the classroom. Literature is a shared event, which means that students and teachers talk and debate with each other, exchanging ideas and creating a community of learners, which includes the teachers. Each is a thoughtful, problem-posing practitioner, and they bring out these characteristics in their students as well.

• Each values authentic forms of learning and assessment that center on student voice, learning, and self-representation.

• The *Teaching Harry Potter* teachers do not ascribe to stereotypes (labeling as a "nerd," "dumb," "retarded," etc.) and push their students to move beyond these connotations in their self-perception and views of others.

- Each embraces popular culture and technology and uses it *wisely*. *Harry Potter* is only one example of what these teachers welcome (and put to work) in their classrooms. They would be even more open to utilizing and developing twenty-first-century learners/ing if they had the autonomy (see the first point above) and infrastructure, including technology, to do so. These teachers are not afraid to try new things and risk innovation. They are not afraid to imagine more for their students.

- Each teacher is resilient. They adapt to changing circumstances and the unique challenges of their school community (language, curriculum, socioeconomic status, etc.). They also adapt to changing mandates placed upon them by their school, district, and the state (regardless of the teachers' views on these) and work to help their students adapt and cope as well.

- Each is willing to reflect and share their class and curricular outcomes and experience with others at their local school sites, and also in collaboration with researchers and other teachers through published works, such as *Teaching Harry Potter*. While each has taken on some kind of leadership role at the school, they would expand that activity should the proper supports be put in place. Ongoing reciprocal relationships are welcomed and supported in these teachers' working lives.

In examining this list, we look to the *Teaching Harry Potter* teachers and their examples to suggest reframing the oft-posed question of what it is that students *can do* to instead ask what is it that students *experience* in a particular teacher's classroom? In addition, how do these experiences then create rich learning environments where learning is deep and meaningful? What is the experience of curriculum, reading, discussion, and caring? How do the students reflect and utilize the understanding that they have gained as members of a particular classroom community? How are they changed in positive ways by what they learn and accomplish? A central question in our framework, rarely posed in policy mandates, is simply: does the students' learning belong to them? Do they own it? Do they then have the freedom to use their experiences to further their own understanding of the world around them?

Of course, the qualities described above are not measurable. In a data-driven climate, this makes advocacy for such professional attributes rather difficult. We would argue, however, that this current climate makes such advocacy more vital. If we as a society truly want skilled, smart teachers in our schools, then we must offer them more thoughtful—and thought-*provoking*— spaces in which to work. It is time to take more seriously the question of who becomes a teacher in the United States and who we *want* to become teachers. In turn, we also must consider the question of how we can get to the point where those we want to teach actually want to join the profession as well. We have to establish a way of talking and thinking about teaching that would in turn enhance and retain outstanding teachers. There are many impediments to this, including a lack of resources, excellent school leadership, quality mentorship, and support systems for developing teachers.[26] Another significant obstacle lies in the testing system that currently drives so much of curriculum and assessment. Educational historian Diane Ravitch, in her recent book *The Death and Life of the Great American School System,* critiques the system of which she had been a forceful proponent and ponders a similar question regarding her favorite childhood teacher:

> Would any school today recognize her ability to inspire her students to love literature?...I don't think so. She was a great teacher. But under any imaginable compensation scheme, her greatness as a teacher—her ability to inspire students and to change their lives— would go unrewarded because it is not in demand and cannot be measured. And let's face it: She would be stifled not only by the data mania of her supervisors, but by the jargon, the indifference to classical literature and the hostility to her manner of teaching that now prevail in our schools...As we expand the rewards and compensation for teachers who boost scores in basic skills, will we honor those teachers who awaken in their students a passionate interest in history, science, the arts, literature and foreign language?...Will our schools encourage the innovative thinkers who advance society? It's not likely.[27]

Note that Ravitch uses terms such as "inspire," "change," "passionate," and "innovative" to make her point. None of these is present in the NCLB Act's narrow descriptors for a "highly qualified teacher," which includes "(1) a bachelor's degree, (2) full state certification or licensure, and (3) prove that they know each subject they teach."[28] While there is room within the law for states to define what it means "to know the subject they teach," this is likely geared toward veteran teachers who entered the profession before the NCLB Act came into place, as a means to certify that population rather than to expand upon immeasurable qualities such as "innovative." Unfortunately, it also aims at a lowest common denominator for content knowledge. If we were to interview principals, they would likely tell us that they would love to hire passionate, inspirational, and innovative expert teachers. The question is, are these teachers willing to come to work at a particular school, and will they be willing to stay given the limiting teaching climate? Again, this tension is heightened in resource-stripped urban schools. As teaching expert Linda Darling-Hammond states, "Although No Child Left Behind's 'highly qualified teacher' requirement has reduced the hiring of utterly untrained teachers in some states, it has not included support to make well-prepared teachers and leaders available in the neediest communities."[29]

Certainly, some form of standards and reasonable testing (as opposed to high-stakes testing that holds punitive measures for failure) used to inform teachers, students, and their families of progress should play a role in education. When such efforts become the sole focus of the curriculum, however, the educational experience is severely limited at all levels. At this point in time, the Obama administration readies to reauthorize the NCLB Act and Secretary of Education Arne Duncan recently acknowledged that the current assessment system fails "... to test higher-order reasoning and writing skills and thus fail[s] to show what students know and can do." He then goes on to add that "One-shot, year-end bubble tests administered on a single day can lead to dummying down curriculum and instruction throughout the course of the school year."[30] Duncan then proposes the creation of new standards tests that take critical thinking and improved curriculum into account. Such acknowledgment is certainly welcome, but the revised mandates he describes still rely heavily on standardized testing as the primary form of assessment.

The concept around expanding the scope of such tests is reminiscent of the California Learning Assessment System (CLAS) testing of the early 1990s, where students utilized critical thinking skills to answer open-ended questions, sometimes even after being allowed to work in discussion groups, on given reading materials. These were based on the state's frameworks, which at that time were geared toward problem solving. The highly performance-based CLAS tests were administered only for two years because of "technical quality and public credibility concerns."[31] Some parents found the reading selections questionable (they were more oriented to popular texts), and both the administration and scoring of the tests were considered highly subjective. Some questioned the qualifications of those administering and scoring the tests. How will Arne Duncan and his team handle similar issues? Any standardized assessments administered on such a large scale would need to be able to be scored quickly and would have to be perceived as "objective" as well. To retain large-scale credibility in the current political environment, they would also need to be directly linked to state and/or federal standards. All these will likely limit the degree to which any new test can truly capture and reflect a student's critical thinking skills, which are highly individualized and contextualized. We remain hopeful, but guarded.

There are schools that manage, through targeted reform programs, to utilize authentic learning as a form of assessment. Many of these are charter schools, which have more leeway to innovate, as shall be evident in Andrew's case presented in Chapter 4. Darling-Hammond details some of the assessment events utilized at school sites employing authentic evaluation and describes how such measures, portfolios in particular, are utilized successfully in schools reorganized to support teacher and student development. She states that "the tasks require students to organize information, engage in disciplined inquiry and analysis, communicate orally and in writing, problem solve, and make a cogent presentation before an audience" and describes how "students frequently remarked on how the portfolio experience deepened their understanding."[32]

She then goes on to recount a presentation given by a special education student who "could not be distinguished from a regular education student." His history portfolio focused on "...the role of Japan during World War II, displaying knowledge of the geography of the region and the politics of Japanese imperialism."[33] The student presentations were also made to a panel made up of teachers and peers, highlighting another level of active participation for both groups.

We obviously advocate for creating and supporting school environments that would allow the *Teaching Harry Potter* teachers and their students to flourish in such a manner. Integral to this would be the space to innovate, imagine, and support new possibilities for teaching and learning. This clearly means reducing the impact of the NCLB Act and high-stakes testing on the function and curriculum of schools.

As we narrow and close the spaces once utilized by teachers for exploration of expertise, those who hold it, or the potential to develop excellence, will simply go somewhere else. In the end, much as Dumbledore stated, "it is our choices that show what we truly are."[34] When we as a society choose to limit skilled professionals to the narrowest, most basic forms of their work, with little room for advancement or creativity, then we show clearly how little we believe in the developmental capacity of "good teachers," particularly in high-poverty schools where resources, including teachers, are the most threatened. As a society, we also show that we are unwilling to consider more deeply the long-term ramifications of such policies for the most vulnerable and resource-poor students.

Sandra's account in the following chapter highlights some of the ramifications of these recent policies for her elementary school students, who are primarily Latino English Learners. In describing her work with them, she details what was once possible in her teaching, the reality of her current experience, and how she imagines more and better for her students.

Chapter 2

Harry on the Border between Two Worlds: Reading Harry *en Español* in a Mexican American Border Community*

According to the myth, which has been passed down through the years, Mexican Americans have not really cared for education or else they have failed to appreciate its importance and benefit to their community in particular and to the society at large... new information shows that Mexican Americans have had a deep historical respect for and commitment to education... In many cases the students... later became successful individuals. Some of these individuals became schoolteachers and administrators in public schools...[1]

[When we read Harry Potter] the Latino kids in my class always have the most to say about the books, they are always the most connected...[2]

Native language access in schools remains highly contested. Recent state mandates in Arizona pressuring schools to remove teachers whose English is deemed "heavily accented or ungrammatical"[3] from English Learner classrooms, regardless of the teachers' level of experience and expertise, illustrate the disparaging manner in

---

* Sandra and I grew up in this community, a place where I have done a great deal of research. In the interest of transparency, I introduce the community detailing a research experience that led to the inclusion of this particular teacher and her students in this book.—CLB

which language issues are approached in many districts and states. After the 1998 passage of Proposition 227 in California, which limited access to students' native language to one year, many teachers who had used their students' first language as a bridge to accessing content and gaining confidence in the classroom found these tools unavailable. Coupled with constant pressures from testing mandates at both the federal level (NCLB, No Child Left Behind Act) and the state level (the CAHSEE, or California High School Exit Exam, is a requirement for graduation), immigrant and English Learner students in many states have found their educational opportunities severely narrowed. Often, their curriculum is stripped to the point where content is strictly test-based and delivered through drilling exercises. These children's schooling experiences are thus devoid of opportunities for promoting authentic learning and developing critical thinking, not to mention a robust curriculum that includes science, social studies, and literature.

The first *Teaching Harry Potter* teacher, Sandra, experienced these educational shifts firsthand as a veteran teacher of Mexican immigrant and native Spanish-speaking elementary school children. We both grew up in the town where she has taught elementary school children for 17 years. As a U.S.–Mexico border community, the student population is 98 percent Latino, and bilingualism, biculturalism, and binationalism are the norm. The community also holds an educational history that includes one of the highest graduation rates for Latinos in California. Another distinguishing characteristic of the district is that many of its teachers and administrators are homegrown natives of the town and 85 percent are Latino/a,[4] which means that they hold strong cultural and community connections to the students. Sandra is one of these teachers: bilingual, native-born, and Latina. She is also a teacher I have known and worked with for many years. I have spent time in her classroom, and we have had many cups of coffee together discussing her experiences and philosophy of education.

During one of our conversations, I related an experience I had trying to find a copy of *Harry Potter and the Goblet of Fire* in the town's library.[5] Where four copies should have been in place, there were none. As a matter of fact, where more than a dozen copies of all then published *Potter* books should stand, stood only a single copy of *Chamber of Secrets*.[6] Stunned, I had to admit to having been genuinely surprised to find the books checked out. In past experience and research, fantasy books and books of that length in English had been a tough sell for border-town kids. Obviously, I had allowed familiarity with the site to lead me to make assumptions about cultural practice, thus breaking a cardinal rule of observational research.

In many ways, the experience made perfect sense. *Harry Potter* is a worldwide phenomenon; of course, children, and adults, would be curious. Given its widespread popularity, the novels' appeal definitely crossed boundaries of culture, language, and nationality. However, in thinking more closely on the content of the novels, cultural differences such as Harry being a white, British boy became less important than the ways in which Harry's experiences, and the magical elements of his story, could actually serve to draw in rather than alienate many Latino and Latino immigrant readers.

For example, in many schools and communities, magic and "witchcraft" often form the base for banning the *Potter* books altogether. Yet, the presence of "magic" is the norm in much of Latin American literature. Magical realism is a classic genre that includes some of the world's greatest works, such as Marquez' *One Hundred Years of Solitude*.[7] While not exactly the same, forms of "magic," spirits, parallel worlds, healers, and mystical guides, permeate Latin American culture and books. Rudolfo Anaya's *Bless Me Ultima*,[8] long considered a classic of Chicano (Mexican American) literature, is often required reading in advanced English and university courses. It is also a boy's (Antonio) coming of age story, much like Harry's. Both stories are saturated with magical power and events of various types. In Antonio's world, which is of our own as opposed to Rowling's parallel world, magic permeates life. Here lies an excellent example of Latin magical realism, whereby magic is incorporated into the everyday life and therefore seems naturally occurring. Saldivar describes how Anaya "…leads his readers through an enchanting, mystical landscape, animated by spiritual forces that seem to affect the course of personal destiny" and how Antonio "looks not to history but to myth, magic, ritual, and symbol as the sources of the stuff of life and as the context of his growth..."[9] Harry would certainly feel comfortable in this world.

The border-crossing aspects of Harry's experience are also valuable here. In many ways, Harry is an immigrant himself. At the age of 11, he crosses the barrier/border into a new world that while welcoming is also formidable. He must learn how to navigate a new culture (norms, values, cultural cues), and in many instances, particularly in school, a new language (terminology). Harry accomplishes this while keeping an eye out for those who seek to harm or "capture" him, an effort that becomes increasingly exhausting as Harry comes of age and realizes the true seriousness of his situation. These experiences of newness, isolation, cultural miscues as well as joy at discovery, abiding friendship, and personal growth are key points that can serve to guide comparisons with Harry's story. Children and adults can relate to him, even if they do not share his background. However, familiar cultural elements, mostly based in a similar folkloric tradition, and perhaps an immigration experience, may facilitate this for Latino kids and communities.

Harry Potter's popularity, engaging storytelling, and cultural resonance might explain the lack of controversy and apparent acceptance of the novels in the community. However, many questions remained. Were students reading the books in school? If so, what did that look like and how were the children responding to the text? I posed these questions, and Sandra told me that she had actually read *Harry Potter and the Sorcerer's Stone*[10] with one of her second-grade classes and that it had gone really well. The reading took place during her tenth year of teaching, when she was still assigned traditional bilingual education classes. Given our numerous discussions around the event and her thoughtful approach when describing her students' reactions to the text, the reading clearly serves as one of her most formative teaching experiences.

The read-aloud, which took place over the course of two months, goes against all current policies and trends focused on Mexican American and immigrant education in the United States: Sandra read the novel in Spanish, she did not utilize pacing guides or standardized periodic assessments, and students asked questions and dialogued about the story in Spanish, English, and/or both languages.

(She notes that some students in this Bilingual class were transitioning to English and, in an attempt to master their new language, spoke in English whenever they were cognitively able.)

All one needs do is listen to the rhetoric put forth regarding immigrants and bilingualism in this country to know that we do not expect a great deal from these populations, let alone that a class of Spanish-dominant second graders would sit, over the course of many hours, engaged and attentive while their teacher read to them. As Sandra stated, "As if immigrant were synonymous with incapable." If we did believe that these students could accomplish more, we would certainly eliminate the scripted, remedial programs that often bind them, and so many other students of color, to a rote education.

Given that Latino youth are the fastest growing school population, yet they have one of the highest dropout/pushout rates, this issue is of vital concern. As Latino students of all backgrounds generally enter school with enthusiasm, U.S. schools are obviously not meeting their needs.[11] Those who study the Latino educational experience in the United States seeking to elaborate on the means to improve schooling for Latino students overall point to cultural awareness and acceptance on the part of educators, access to one's native language, and quality academic programs (that exhibit high expectations) as key supports to Latino student success.[12] In addition, active role models and points in the curriculum with which students can readily identify allow for entrance into the classroom dialogue as active participants.[13] Current school policy does not focus on any of these points, for any group of students.

In 2001, Sandra and her class of "bilingual" (transitioning to English) second graders engaged in open, unscripted dialogue based in the reading of a complete novel. Sandra read aloud and students listened, engaged over the course of many hours, days, and weeks. The students asked questions based in the story, yet connected to their own lives, and were clearly invested in the experience. Curiosity, critical thought, and open discourse were the hallmarks of this shared, essentially community-story, experience. While clearly a highlight of her teaching career, she has not been able to replicate the experience primarily because of curricular changes brought about by the NCLB Act.

Sandra's narrative is constructed from a combination of interviews, discussions, and coauthorship. She begins with a reflection on her thought processes and the discussion between her and her students as they made the decision about the book that she would read with them as an end-of-the-year activity:

> The year I read *Sorcerer's Stone* with my students, I personally had only read the first *Harry Potter* book in English. I didn't read them all until book six had been released years later and then I read them all that summer. I thought the books sounded "neat," but once the movies came out, they seemed more interesting. Once I read them, the books were pleasant surprises. It's just really great to get all of the minor and edited details; you know, the ones the screenwriters leave out of the movie. In the end, you miss out on so much if you only rely on the movie.
>
> I began reading *Sorcerer's Stone* toward the end of the year, so there were no grades or assignments. I just read to them for the sake of enjoyment. I really wanted it to be something they would remember and, being a teacher, hoped it would create a love of good stories and of course lifelong readers. I told the students that I wanted to read a chapter book to them, I said "I'm going to share a story with you." It was toward the end of the school year, so I told them that they would need to work hard at their CST [California Standards Test] review sessions all morning, but that in the afternoon, they would get to hear a really cool story. (Okay, so I used a little bribery.) In a nutshell, that's why I decided to do it. I felt that some of the kids I had this particular year could really benefit from a story being read aloud to them. Some of them were straight from Mexico, and this activity would be all oral so they wouldn't have to worry about writing anything down. This was really important given that some of these same students were almost as "barren" in their native language as they were in English. When I read aloud, the students didn't have to worry about pronunciation or having to read to understand, so the anxiety level was lowered.
>
> I thought about it and realized we could create an open forum as well. We could discuss prediction, character analysis, compare/contrast characters, etc. It sounded like it could really be fun. I also hoped that through hearing and liking the story they would pick up a book on their own. I remember my fourth-grade teacher reading to

us, and she recommended those books to her students. I remember kids who didn't like reading and all it took was one book to change that way of thinking.

The first *Harry Potter* movie was being released at that time and a couple of my students had *Harry Potter and the Sorcerer's Stone* and were trying to read it, in Spanish. They were struggling. I asked, "How many of you would like me to read *Harry Potter* to you?" And most kids reacted positively. They had wanted to read it themselves, but could not understand a lot of the vocabulary.

So, I started at the beginning.

I told the class that every day I would read one chapter of *Sorcerer's Stone*. I also warned them that it would not sound like the typical Spanish they hear, it would be more formal. I also knew reading the whole book and working through the vocabulary was going to be work on my part. I actually thought I wouldn't finish it, that the kids would get bored, but that didn't happen.

A lot of time went into reading the book; we had to talk about it a lot. I read it in Spanish, but felt *Harry Potter* gave the students a chance to connect with this "other" English culture they were living in because they could connect with the kids and school in the book. Potter provided a way to connect with a friendly English environment. The bilingual class is a bubble, and many were going to transition to English the next year, which can be scary. Our class was also safe because I speak Spanish, and no one was going to tell them "you have to speak English!" They needed to make a connection to the English-speaking world, though, and I thought this book could help them.

The book also gave me perfect opportunities to connect to their world and language. For example, I commented to them about differences in movie dubbing/translations [when the translation doesn't quite match the original dialogue]. Sometimes the book translation was different as well, and I pointed that out, reminding them the author wrote in English, and then I would give the students a more specific translation. This is especially true of the idioms and colloquialisms.

I also wanted their first real experience with a novel and/or chapter book to be something good and positive. They were going to relate to *Harry Potter* for sure, I mean, they're kids, and doing magic is something they have all fantasized about, wishing they had powers. Going to school was also relatable. Although they didn't understand the boarding school concept, one student made the comment, "they sleep there?" I had to explain that some kids leave home to go to school and only see their families during vacation. A lot of the students said they wouldn't want to do that, some wouldn't want to leave their family, but they did want to go to Hogwarts. When Harry goes back to the Dursley's, for example, where he's not loved, the students noticed that all the other Hogwarts kids were looking forward to going home, but not Harry. He'd rather be there [school] than home, so the kids talked about that. They decided they would want to go home, but agreed they would not go with the Dursleys, "they're so mean to him" [Harry]. They asked: "Why doesn't he just go live somewhere else, he has money?" I had to explain that the Dursleys were his guardians by law. I didn't know at that time that Dumbledore had made the arrangement with Petunia [to keep and thus protect Harry until age 17].

As Sandra's narrative indicates, her interaction with her students was open not only to their Spanish language base but also to the personal connections that they made with her; the trust that they placed in Sandra enabled them to ask clarifying questions about the story and to participate readily in book conversations. Anxieties around their ability or need to speak English were lessened and thus did not prevent them from actively participating. They were able to lower what linguist Stephen Krashen terms their "affective filters,"[14] which can inhibit learning under stressful circumstances. As educator Lisa Delpit states, "the less stress and the more fun connected to the process, the more easily it is accomplished."[15] Such learning events are clearly evident in Sandra's account.

Angela Valenzuela describes the disconnect that many Latino students feel toward U.S. educational systems as also stemming from the school's "subtraction" of their culture, which values "the opportunity to engage in reciprocal relationships" as an integral aspect of education.[16] Clearly, Sandra's experience supports the notion of an "additive" educational experience based in a reciprocity that gave the students open access to her as a teacher and an approachable mentor. She welcomed their contributions, and supported their home and school languages. Given the opportunity, proper supports, and encouragement, Spanish-dominant, second-grade students can engage in forms of discourse usually reserved for older students and/or advanced English courses.

It is critical to look at what was, and could still be, accomplished under more open circumstances when curricular choice was actually an option. Under the guidance of a culturally "attuned" teacher who practices Ladson-Billings's culturally relevant pedagogy,[17] such choices become particularly powerful. By attuned, one does not necessarily mean sharing the same cultural background, but being open to the cultural practice and sensibility of the community in which one works. Given that Sandra is an insider, she holds such awareness organically; it is part of her and her school experience. However, as Ladson-Billings notes, culturally relevant teaching is based in perceptions, beliefs, and relationships:

> They [teachers] see themselves as a part of the community and they see teaching as giving back to the community. They help students make connections between their local, national, racial, cultural, and global identities. Such teachers can also be identified by the ways in which they structure their social interactions: Their relationships with students are fluid and equitable and extend beyond the classroom. They demonstrate a connectedness with all of their students and encourage a community of learners; they encourage their students to learn collaboratively.[18]

It is also important to note that Sandra did not lower her expectations for her students. They were still working toward state exams. They were still expected to participate in the reading project by asking questions and paying attention. In many ways, since Sandra opened the door to multiple forms of expression, she expected more and richer contributions from her students. She also used the students' media access, primarily to the first movie, to help them connect more readily to the story. While sometimes the movie served as a guide, it also served as a point of contrast to talk about why changes had been made, or, as previously stated, the language differed. Of note is the fact that while none of the students had read the first Potter book on their own, most of the class had seen the movie. Sandra used that to illuminate the reading and class discussion.

The level of student engagement that developed as Sandra continued to read the novel grew to such a degree that she was able to utilize it fully as a learning tool. The class discussed language (formal and informal), character development, and morals. Simultaneously, Sandra worked to enhance the kids' concentration and auditory skills, develop their critical thinking, and grow her students' confidence as students. The form and content of the kids' questions to her served as the assessments, enabling her to gauge their progress. As the students heard more of the story, their participation increased and they asked to be read to in longer sittings. Sandra recounts this development and the students' fear that they would not have time to finish the book:

> When I first began reading, many students did not understand what was happening in the story. Even though we were reading in Spanish, the book is written at a fourth/fifth-grade reading level, so there were many words the students hadn't heard before. They didn't necessarily use formal or academic vocabulary at home. I wanted them to understand the story, what the words meant, and what was happening. So, as I read, I paused to teach. As I read the first chapter, I asked clarification questions, "What does that mean?" for example. The kids would also ask me questions and we then had oral discussions. Sometimes someone had missed something or wanted me to clarify events. I mean, they were seven and eight years old.
>
> Part of why I decided to read *Sorcerer's Stone* aloud was because there were a couple of students in that class that had been identified as RSP (Resource Specialist Program), but I also had a group of kids who were ready to transition into the traditional English class the next year so they were pretty capable in English. I was a little wary as to whether all the kids would be able to grasp the content, plus it's a long book. It took over a month and a half to finish. It was a risk, but I had a good relationship with them, I think they trusted me; they were willing to do it and were willing to be patient. I told them, "It will get exciting so just wait" and then they got into the story.
>
> After a week, some lower (reading) level students who seemed distracted and a little bored to that point began sitting up and paying more attention. After about Chapter 5, they started getting into it, and when I finished reading the chapter for the day, they began to ask, "That's it? Can't you read another one?" So, I started reading two chapters, taking at least an hour each time. It was the end of the year, so I felt I could do this.
>
> The girls wanted to be Hermione. They liked that she was smart, and they admired her, but they didn't think they could actually be her, that they could be really smart and know English. They had seen the

movie and saw that she spoke English. While this is a common fear among English Language Learners, I was quick to point out that in just a few years, they too would be speaking in English. I shared with them stories about previous students who had come to my class not knowing any English, but when those same students came to visit me two or three years later, they only spoke to me in English. Imagine the smiles that information produced on their little faces! The boys wanted to be Harry or Ron or Malfoy, some of them thought he [Malfoy] was cool. So then we'd have those types of "social conversations," about a character that is purposely being evil, and how you relate to that. I asked them if they thought that purposely being evil was "cool," but they talked more about Malfoy's character as presented in the movie, that he was rich, etc. and I think they connected to that. In the end, they all agreed that being evil was not the best choice.

We also talked about where the story was taking place; some thought Hogwarts was real, they would ask, "Is that really there?" I told them that the story took place in an English setting, but that Hogwarts didn't exist. The students often asked questions about what was real in the story, again, they were second graders, and all of them wanted it to be real so they could go to Hogwarts.

I also used the movie as a reference, asking, "Remember when in the movie…?" and tried to have them make connections back to the novel, which worked because most of them had seen the movie. Halfway through the book, though, they started getting upset because they felt cheated by the film. They would stop me to ask, "How come that wasn't in the movie? Why didn't they put that it in?" Most kids this age think that the book is written after the movie and so they wanted to know why the author had put in extra events or changed the outcome of a scene, etc. I told them that the book came first; therefore the foundation for the book is better, more detailed. I explained that if the director put everything in the movie it would be too long and told them "Look at how long it's taking me to read it!" I also used the movie to help with visualizing and comparing/contrasting events. I asked them, "Picture the scene I just read to you. Did it happen like that in the movie? How is it different or similar?"

I knew they were learning through the questions they asked me; their questions helped me know whether they understood what was going on. For example, some of the kids didn't understand the story when we began. They didn't understand that Harry slept in a cupboard under the stairs. Students asked me, "Why is the space so small?" I explained to them that Harry was sleeping in a cupboard, which is just a small, little closet space. They reacted strongly to that, some said, "Oh! I thought it was a bedroom." So, I used comments such as those, from the students and myself, to guide moments for clarification. I also continued to ask them questions as we went along. I used the character's dialogue, for example. If a character said something unusual (for example, Hermione is a "Mudblood") and the students asked me to clarify, I would comment and clarify for them.

Toward the end of the book and school year, the students grew upset that we might not finish the book. So I started spending the last three to four hours of school each day reading aloud just to finish. They had no trouble listening. On the next to the last day of school I promised to spend whatever time I could the next day reading. If I hadn't started reading two chapters a day earlier on, we would never have finished. We finished reading *Sorcerer's Stone* on the last day of school. Some were disappointed. They didn't want it to end. Once I cleared up the fact that the other books picked up where the first book left off, they were more accepting. In the end, they all clapped and cheered. "¡Que chilo!" [cool] was heard from various students while others said, "That was so cool, I'm gonna read the next book during vacation."

On that day, some of the kids told me they would read *Chamber of Secrets* over the summer and I told them to make sure they had someone there to help them with it. I don't know how many actually read it, though I remember one student coming back the following year and telling me he had read book two and was going to start the third one in fourth grade.

As the most experienced teacher of the three case study teachers presented here, Sandra is the only one who taught previous to the implementation of the NCLB Act, and worked during the inception and growth of the accountability movement, including the emergence of the California High School Exit Exam (CAHSEE), throughout the mid to late 1990s. During this initial period, curricular standards and accountability assessments were not so rigidly defined. Darling-Hammond states:

> In many cases, these assessments asked students to analyze texts and information in a variety of formats; write persuasive essays and literary critiques; find, evaluate, synthesize, and use information; conduct and present the results of scientific investigations;

and solve complex mathematical problems in real-world settings, showing their solution strategies and explaining their
reasoning.[19]

Sandra's district reflected this trend and implemented many progressive elements during the mid to late 1990s, including thematic
units at the elementary level and the Senior Project at the high
school, a long-term project that involved a lengthy written paper,
an oral presentation (in English or Spanish), and community service requirements.[20] During this period, although the emphasis on
"accountability" continued to grow, critical thinking and reading
were still welcome components in the curriculum.

As accountability mandates became more rigid, however, schools
faced serious challenges to their autonomy and agency. Not producing satisfactory test scores or not meeting your required Academic
Performance Index (API) meant that your school could be labeled as
"failing" and punitive measures would be put in place. Sandra's primarily homegrown district (a significant percentage of teachers and
administrators grew up in the community) had historically defined
success on a local level. Locally established success parameters,
including graduation, getting a job, and college matriculation, were
consistently accomplished in striking numbers.[21] However, severe
external pressures brought on by the NCLB Act and the CAHSEE
forced the district to alter its focus toward raising test scores. Given
the high poverty and large immigrant population, such external
exams had historically proven challenging for the school district as a
whole. Under NCLB's mandates, however, these challenges became
much more threatening.

Passage of Proposition 227 (anti-bilingual legislation) in 1998
also affected the district a great deal. The bilingual program, long
an integral part of the district, was cut back to serve only those students whose parents signed waivers requesting that they remain in
a bilingual education classroom. Reading in Spanish, therefore, was
limited to these spaces. Today, classroom functioning in the district,
centered on scripted curriculums and Explicit Direct Instruction
(EDI) with the aim of raising test scores, is almost unrecognizable
from that of 15 years ago.

Sandra's *Teaching Harry Potter* story, therefore, reflects both the beginnings of the *Harry Potter* phenomenon and the emerging/ongoing effects of the accountability and standards movements on education in the community. Given the Latino, primarily Mexican American demographics, and the high immigrant population (again, largely Mexican), her experience offers us much to think on with regard to Latino educational access and potential in U.S. schools. This history is incredibly important, particularly to any discussion regarding the value of teacher autonomy and decision making (choice). What is the value of structuring the curriculum to meet the needs of a particular community of students? What is the value of a skilled teacher who can do this work, if given the space to make intuitive decisions based in experience and expertise?

Sandra's experience also says much about cultural gatekeeping and who holds the keys. Her then second-grade students were obviously excited about the "new" Harry Potter phenomenon. However, they had trouble accessing the books in terms of language and reading level. While still able to share in Harry Potter's growing cultural presence through movies and Spanish film translations, Sandra's students faced barriers of language and reading level in their attempt to read the books themselves. Recognizing this, Sandra helped them navigate through that process, in essence, providing the keys to successfully engaging the literary component. While such intuitive awareness is the hallmark of any good teacher, Sandra's ability to both role model and naturally recognize the inherent difficulties of such a process lend a fluidity to her approach. Unfortunately, some of her keys have been, in essence, confiscated.

Although it has become difficult, Sandra still works to create spaces where she can read aloud and thus "share stories" with her students. Unfortunately, these experiences are often rushed or limited (by time), but she continues to push to create such opportunities whenever possible. More often, though, she laments the loss of time to engage in critical discussions with her students:

> After that year, I kept the *Harry Potter* books in my classroom, but I never had a chance to read them again. Things started changing with the curriculum, the school really started counting instructional minutes and reading a book aloud wasn't something I could do in a

week. For the past two years, since we've been using EDI, it's been nearly impossible to even imagine trying to get something like that done. There have been so many changes, and the time isn't there and we [teachers] are watched like hawks. About four years ago, we [the school] came to the point where the administration said we should all be on the same page at the same time. So if one of them walks into the classroom and you're not on script...

At this point, there's a scripted program for everything, and you better follow the pacing guide. I understand there are teachers out there who don't work and may need watching, but this type of curriculum ties the hands of those of us who are working. We're also robbing students of a "full" education that exposes them to things other than ten-page stories in an anthology. Glimpses of "this and that" aspects of a story do not provide a well-rounded program. And since the reading exercises are so scripted, there is very little opportunity to think on one's own, to reach one's own conclusions, or form an opinion on anything. There's no time for dialogue around any questions the students might need to ask.

For example, as we read *Sorcerer's Stone*, there were so many opportunities to ask, "What would you have done if that happened to you? So and so had no choice, what would you have done?" A scene as simple as when Malfoy steals Neville's Remembrall gave me the opportunity to ask, "Why did he do that? Why do you think he did it? Is Malfoy just mean, or is he jealous? Maybe he wants to look good or prove he's funny." The characters in the novel are more rounded than the flat characters presented in anthologies where we have no background story. We have too little information to truly know the characters, so therefore we can't reach conclusions about their motivation or desires.

Had I been able to read all seven *Harry Potter* books, it would have been exciting to explore how Harry changed over time, but also how he doesn't change at all. Harry could easily have become a Malfoy, but he doesn't change who he is; Harry's essential core, those qualities that make him special, remain. Even in the beginning, through the first book, he could have reacted differently when he found out he had money, or he could have walked around saying "I'm the one who defeated You-Know-Who" but he never did.

Under the current curriculum, "character traits" is a California teaching standard, but the students are given so few opportunities to see any characters in action that it's a difficult idea for them to internalize. The kids can't see how a particular character is selfish, for example, from a short book excerpt in an anthology. They can't then make decisions about the character's motivation if they don't have the necessary evidence to form a conclusion. And this is vitally important because the students then don't know how to make thoughtful decisions about each other. For example, one student in the class may have "ugly" clothes, or what the kids consider "no sense of style," but maybe the reason is the student's family is poor and that hasn't been considered. Now, though, the kids don't ask "Why?" Where are they going to practice this skill, this way of thinking, if they're not studying other people's experiences in this imaginary world of books?

This has been the worst year for reading as far as my being able to interact with a story. At the beginning of the year, I picked a few short picture books to read aloud, and I enjoyed that. I also managed to read one simple chapter book. It was part of a series, and I could tell that these kids would have enjoyed *Harry Potter* if we could have read it. Once I began reading to them, they started to ask daily, "You're going to read to us, aren't you?"

I wanted to do more reading this year, but I couldn't work it in. I can't read any additional novels or excerpts because of the new policies. We have standards and standards pacing guides with tests for the kids every week, plus benchmark tests every six weeks and every twelve weeks an Essential Standards test. The students are bored; at the beginning, it is fun for them because it's so predictable and they can all follow along. After a while, though, the really bright kids say "I can do it myself" and I can make that work with some of the curriculum, but not with everything. Others just say they are bored and ask why they have to do this.

The whole morning is spent going through the pacing guide conducting 30-minute EDI lessons, and then we have ELD (English Language Development), lunch, math, and social studies. There's also RTI (Response to Intervention) time where teachers switch kids then teach "Standards Plus." Given this schedule, I even have a hard time teaching the short, edited stories in the anthologies! I mean, when am I going to get the story in? Forget literature, there is no literature. Kids got most of their reading this year from AR (Accelerated Reader). The students in more advanced levels read [AR] chapter books. If somebody happens to pick up *Harry Potter*,

I ask them what chapter they're on and about different events in the books, asking "Wasn't that cool when . . ."

In Accelerated Reader, the kids read books to pass computerized tests, not to find out about how other people live, battle their own demons and come out okay, or how other people "did that," accomplished their goal. If the students do have a chance to learn something important like that, they don't remember it for long. So much emphasis is placed on tests and competition, and we end up pushing that along, encouraging it, as teachers. The kids are reading, but they're reading for tests; actually many are mostly reading for pizza [schools provide parties for students scoring at grade/reading level on all tests]. AR then also causes some students to develop a fear of moving to the next reading level [because they are afraid they won't pass the tests]. This makes them afraid to try to move up and read more difficult books.

As a result of these changes, student exposure is limited to simplistic stories, which they have few problems understanding. The minute it gets complicated, they get lost. In life, there is complexity, and the students are not exposed to that reality. For example, this year we read a story called "Trapped by the Ice" and I had to intervene and read it to them. It wasn't like any of their other anthology stories; it was nonfiction, longer, and in journal form. The vocabulary was more advanced too, some of it they hadn't seen before. The top student got a 90 percent on the initial assessment, she missed one question, so I figured three to four others could do well. One student got an 80, then another a 70, so I grew concerned. I asked the class how many of them were having trouble and hands went up, some hesitantly.

I explained that this was one of the more difficult stories in the book, and that it was okay if they were having a hard time. After reassuring them, I asked again about needing help and practically all their hands went up. The students told me the story was confusing, they didn't know what was happening. I connected the reading to their own journals they write in during class, telling them that the man [narrator] in the story was keeping a record of his journey. One student asked, "Oh, you mean it really happened? How did they know what happened [that long ago]?" I explained that we know because this man kept a journal, and it was used to write the story. I then read it to them aloud in parts, pausing after I'd read a section to ask questions in order to get them thinking. Toward the end, they were reading and asking questions and were able to understand. Their scores varied, but all of them got the gist of the story, they understood what happened to the author.

The Huffington Post recently published an article about the lasting effects of the *Harry Potter* books from the viewpoint of librarians of the New York City Public Library (NYCPL).[22] They describe how influential the books have been not only in getting children to read but also in increasing kids' interest in science, history, and mythology. It turns out that the librarians run a science program called "Snape's Lab" that has been very popular and has "all sorts of chemical potions... The kids just really like that part. The chemistry." They also discuss the multigenerational and family aspects of sharing the books, particularly since they are accessible in so many languages:

> I remember one time when a kid came over and he told me he wanted *Harry Potter* but he wanted it in Chinese. He's come before and he only reads stuff in English, so I asked him why he wanted it in Chinese. He said, "Yeah, my grandma wants it. She saw me reading it and now she's reading it."[23]

While not a school event, the story connects to Sandra's experience, of sharing the stories through the language of family and home. It reminds one that these parallel events, or reading at school and reading at home, should be closer, if not overlapping. One thinks again of the public library in Sandra's school community and wonders whether there is a similar story to be told there.

Another really interesting point that the librarians bring out is that they have had some success, albeit limited, trying to find other books for *Harry Potter* fans to read. In their experience, the most successful of these to date is Rick Riordan's *Percy Jackson* series, which also introduces many children to Greek mythology. In helping kids make their reading choices, one characteristic that the librarians find is not an issue with post-Potter readers is the fact that they are no longer intimidated by "big" books. One librarian states, "I'll say, 'You know, that one's kind of long,' and they'll [kids] respond, 'Oh, that's OK, I read all the *Harry Potter* books.' So kids are not afraid or intimidated by longer books, which is good."[24]

Aside from reading *Percy Jackson*, the trends described by the NYCPL librarians are not shared by Sandra's current students. While some of her students are reading, and *The Lightning Thief*[25] (the first book in the *Percy Jackson* series) and *Diary of a Wimpy Kid*[26] are among those students' favorites, Sandra is careful to point out that, as her account describes, she is not able to provide the support and reader modeling that she has seen make a significant difference in students' view of what literature is accessible to them. Without rich classroom reading events, in either English or Spanish, there is little opportunity to build reader confidence and stamina among her students. They are simply not used to reading books or stories of significant length and are therefore intimidated by longer books:

> Two years ago, I had a student who loved to read, she picked out *Sorcerer's Stone* from the library and read it pretty quickly. I asked her if she liked it and she answered with an enthusiastic "yeah!" She had picked up the book herself, and then read all but the last one by the end of the year. I asked if she was going to read the last book over the summer and she said yes. I saw her later the following year, and she'd read it. I actually wondered if she was ready to read the later books, but didn't want to interfere with that. I felt a lot might have gone over her head, particularly many of the darker sequences that a young mind would probably not relate to just yet. She was a very bright third grader, and there are definitely things in the books young students can decode and understand. However, they're young and see the books at a certain level, whereas we see them at an adult level. I didn't want to push the books on her, though. I wanted her to continue on her own. She was a natural reader, although she did take the AR points.
>
> This past year, one student read *Sorcerer's Stone*, but she didn't go on to the next book. I think sometimes they see the movies and the kids get disappointed at the differences in the books. They don't see that the movie comes from the book, they think it's the other way around, and they sometimes get turned off. We had a conversation like the one I had with my second-grade class about why the movie would be too long and the director needed to take only the most important parts, but I got the idea that she wanted the book to be like the movie. Another problem is the kids see how thick the books

are and that's it. They're third-grade ELs (English Learners) and that makes it intimidating.

Kids who love to read will read regardless, but I'm hoping they'll start to read to understand, rather than compete to answer five questions on a computer exam. I'm hoping that through constantly encouraging them to read more, those who are also then pushed at home will read. However, the others have to get it somewhere, they have to get it from me. In that, I haven't done enough. Professionally, within the curriculum constraints, I have, but personally, I feel I could do more given the opportunity and freedom.

Sandra's account shows us what is possible. During the reading of *Sorcerer's Stone*, the students came to own their classroom experience. Sandra may have served as the reader, but the students helped control the delivery. They started and stopped the story as needed to pose questions, thus adjusting the pace according to their needs. In one instance, this meant asking for more chapters per reading session, thus speeding up the story delivery. Her students also guided the line of questioning toward the topics that they found important or to which they related, Harry's family life, for example. Their engagement reflects the confidence that they gained with material that they had initially viewed as intimidating. It also shows what comes of high expectations.

Sandra's account forces us to ask what it means for a teacher to have had an experience like reading *Sorcerer's Stone* with her students, to know that it was rewarding, meaningful, and successful on many levels, and not be able to use that experience, to engage such an opportunity fully, again. What does it mean to know better, and to *know how*, but not be allowed to fully utilize and build upon that expertise? What do restrictions on forms of pedagogy and learning also then mean for the agency of teachers as professionals? Most importantly, what are the consequences of these limitations when the students are primarily Latino English Learners who stand to benefit a great deal from such classroom-based experiences? We shall continue to consider these issues as we explore the current school context in the next chapter.

Another Take on Teaching *Harry Potter*: In Defense of a Magic-less World

After a lesson—more of a project—in which my seventh graders identified areas of their community that they wanted to improve, Alma looked rather frustrated. "I wish we could just wave a wand and all the tagging in Watts would be gone," she blurted out. I wasn't too surprised at the comment. Her independent reading book for the month had been *Harry Potter and the Sorcerer's Stone* and she could barely put it down. And from the vantage point of a twelve-year-old, her solution would be a whole lot easier than repainting the graffiti-stained community. I was tempted to reply, "Me too." The reason I didn't, however, was because only a few months earlier at my college graduation I had heard J. K. Rowling give an articulate defense of a magic-less world. "We do not need magic to change the world," she said, "we carry all the power we need inside ourselves already: we have the power to imagine better." In this teachable moment (but really, what moments aren't?), I worked with my students to prove that when we employ imagination not to escape but to engage, we have all the power that a wand could wield. For homework, I had my students write about their ideal community. They didn't write about flying cars (or broomsticks); they wrote about graffiti-free walls, trash-free streets, and violence-free housing projects. Strip away the magic of *Harry Potter* and you have a story about a group of kids trying to create a better world. This, I think, is Rowling's most important message.

Nick
Seventh- and eighth-grade ESL teacher, public middle school, Los Angeles, two years' experience.

Chapter 3

Harry in the Classroom: Waking Sleeping Dragons*

"And what good's theory going to be in the real world?" said Harry loudly...

Professor Umbridge looked up.

"This is school, Mr. Potter, not the real world."[1]

A particularly striking educational moment in the movie version of *Harry Potter and the Order of the Phoenix* occurs during the first meeting of Professor Umbridge's fifth-year Defense Against the Dark Arts (DADA) class. She announces to the students that they will not be practicing spells, but instead learning them through a "...carefully structured, Ministry-approved course of defensive magic."[2] She then proceeds to distribute their new textbooks, which look to be at least 50 years old and highly reminiscent of our "Muggle" elementary school primers *Dick and Jane*.

The students' negative—and argumentative—reaction is predictable. After all, Hogwarts is an experiential school, one where students not only listen to lectures and sit for traditional exams but also engage in spell work, actively mix potions, and interact with magical creatures and magical plants in order to learn to care for

* Hogwarts school motto: Draco dormiens nunquam titillandus (Never tickle a sleeping dragon)

them. Students then also take practical exams to complement their standard counterparts. Importantly, expert members of the larger Wizarding society come to the school and assist in the grading of these practical exams, engaging the community in school events. The idea, then, that students would simply learn through rote memorization and traditional written exams, particularly for a course so based in real-world experiences, seems ridiculous and dangerous in the students' eyes. In ours as well.

In Chapter 1, we have already discussed the students' formation of Dumbledore's Army (DA) in direct response to Umbridge's refusal to engage the practical, experiential aspects of teaching. However, the fact that similar restrictions occur in U.S. classrooms every day deserves a closer look. In a later scene from the movie, the students are shown copying verbatim from the textbooks while Umbridge instructs: "You will please copy the approved text four times to ensure maximum retention. There will be no need to talk…" to which Hermione, ever the discerning student, states, "No need to think is more like it."[3] Were we to poll many students today, it is likely that we would find that many of them have experienced something similar.

In exploring these classroom tensions, it is vitally important to note that Umbridge represents not teachers, but the Ministry and its intrusion into the educational processes of the school. Too often we, as a society, are quick to lay blame on the teachers' doorsteps without considering the larger school environments and policies under which they work. In our discussion of teaching in Chapter 1, we acknowledge that not all teachers are perfect or equally skilled, but must reiterate that their experience, training, and support systems do not always lend themselves to pedagogical innovation, or at least not without a great deal of pushback and pushing on the part of educators. Under the current system, the potential for creating rich teachable moments is often limited by scripted curriculums and assessment structures that, once again, would certainly meet with Umbridge's approval.

Sandra's previous account also reiterates both the possibilities and the challenges of teaching in contemporary U.S. public schools. Hers is a clear example of how external pressures can impact the practice of even a highly skilled, highly knowledgeable, veteran teacher. In turn, it highlights the everyday experience for her students, which has moved from interactive to unshared, rote learning. This chapter brings the student experience into conversation and highlights important questions about how, when, and where active, authentic learning takes place. In considering the school context, we focus on three aspects of U.S. schooling that impact each teachers' work: multicultural school settings, the use and role of popular culture in the classroom, and the desire for improved media literacy in students. As in Chapter 1, we begin our discussion with the way things are and push readers to imagine the way things might be.

Waking Sleeping Dragons

The U.S. schooling system has always reflected the politics of the time period. Structured at the turn of the century by utilizing the emerging factory system as a model (in order to properly sort by ability and age and thus "meet the needs" of large numbers of students in urban centers), various schooling innovations have cycled through schools.[4] Examples include Progressive, child-centered educational practices, such as those we currently see in Montessori preschools, and various reform efforts that have often been implemented in response to competition from other countries, such as when the USSR launched Sputnik in 1957, causing a rush to improve science education in the United States. Schools today reflect the current climate in much the same manner. Unfortunately, this means that much as other public resources such as libraries, they are underresourced while simultaneously much is demanded of them. Given that little has changed in terms of how we schedule the school day, what is offered and required during that day, and how we categorize students as they move through their school experience (college bound, vocational, or remedial), the current school factory also grows increasingly outdated against the backdrop of rapid technology growth and access to information.

As a result, many schools provide neither the educational experiences and resources proven valuable in the past nor the learning environments, tools, and new skills identified as important to the future. Music, art, and physical education have been drastically reduced in many districts (and in some cases removed altogether) in favor of increasing the number of instructional hours focused on preparing students for the literacy and math content that they will encounter on standardized tests. In this instructional environment, higher-order thinking skills, problem solving, critical thinking, and the real-world application of academic, social, media-related, and technical skills have become afterthoughts. Sadly, the poorer students are, the higher their chances that remediated test preparation will dominate the curriculum that they encounter during a school day. For poor students of color in urban schools, this is almost guaranteed.

Teaching *Harry Potter* within the current educational climate in public schools can therefore prove a subversive act on the part of teachers, particularly given the time required to read a complete book. As Sandra indicates, such readings are no longer possible in her classroom given the time constraints around test preparation and the label her students hold as English Learners (ELs), which means that they receive additional test preparation for exams. She is lucky to squeeze in a short book at the beginning or end of the school year. As Allegra and Andrew also discuss in their respective chapters, the choice to introduce a book that is neither a part of their schools' regular reading lists nor a part of their students' regular media diets also presented unique challenges, including questions concerning the value of the book for urban students of color and what happens when students are not allowed to complete the reading experience.

Reading *Harry Potter* can also prove a subversive act for the students in contemporary classrooms. The books can serve as an opportunity to move beyond the standard canon of accepted school works as well as past the sanitized reading excerpts that students encounter in story anthologies and test preparation materials. Instead, much like Sandra's second-grade students, they can move forward to share a meaningful reading experience with their teachers and classmates. This is not to say that reading *Harry Potter* will provide a salient experience for all; but it will provide an experience that students can use to further develop their own reading tastes (likes and dislikes) and also inform the larger world around them as evidenced in Sandra's discussions with her students about boarding schools or what motivates people to make particular choices or behave in certain ways. Without such reading events, students are locked out of not only learning to read critically, but are kept from learning more about themselves as well.

Such constraints leave us with a generally uninspiring portrait of public schooling, one we and the *Teaching Harry Potter* teachers, would like to see change. Milton Chen, author of *Education Nation*, puts forth the idea that those invested in education "must consider the possibility that students are justified in being bored, that we have been too cautious and unimaginative, that we have let our schools stagnate in the backwaters of our national life."[5] Chen then calls attention to the fact that schooling is indeed a system—and one he currently sees as broken. The solution that he proposes involves a commitment to innovation that shows students:

> ...that school is where the action is, intellectually and physically, that the classroom as well as the playfield is a vivid place, a place of adventure and surprise, of manageable ordeals, of belly laughs-a place, in short, of learning...Education is hard work, and that is true. But it is also great fun, an everlasting delight, and sometimes even ecstasy.[6]

The vision that Chen articulates is vastly preferable to the sorting and labeling factory previously described. Certainly, the teachers here hold similar desires for their students and their classroom communities, hoping that learning events are not only instructive but also transformative. In speaking of her concerns for her current students and the limiting school experience that she believes they receive, Sandra wishes that she could show them how "there's a whole world out there and you can start to get it know it through books. Go explore, think about it..." She continues to work to inspire her students, but telling students about great books and actually reading them together are two very different things. Sandra wants to be able to do more.

For those who can read books in school, Harry himself provides powerful inspiration for both teachers and students reconsidering the current culture of schooling. Harry is, arguably, Hogwarts' most famous student, yet his arrival at the school marks the beginning of a sea change within the Wizarding world. From his first day at Hogwarts, he works against numerous Wizarding norms, in many ways unconsciously pushing back against the school's motto, "Never Tickle a Sleeping Dragon." Throughout Harry's time at Hogwarts (as well as after he leaves the school to hunt Horcruxes), he plays a significant part in efforts to awaken and challenge long sleeping "dragons" of Wizarding society—racism, classism, and other instantiations of ignorance. And, although the struggles were difficult and the losses great, the series ends with a reassurance that Hogwarts students and members of the Wizarding world in general are no longer tiptoeing around those sleeping beasts.

What would happen if we took on the "sleeping dragons" of our educational system? What would it take to expose and disempower assumptions about student needs and success—particularly those related to race, class, gender, and ability? How might teachers, students, and other concerned citizens "tickle" the powers-that-be in order to prompt a reimagination of the form and function of schooling? The teachers' stories in this book show how they work daily to answer these questions; there are, undoubtedly, many more engaged in the same task.

As we discussed in detail in Chapter 1, our vision for education is based upon subverting the current movement toward a singular form of educational accountability in favor of one that privileges agency and decision-making power (choice)—on the part of both teachers and students—in our schools. In addition to choice, we advocate a vision of culturally relevant teaching that takes popular culture seriously—as seriously as students do. This vision looks at popular media not as antithetical to literary canon and the cadre of vetted knowledge that makes up traditional curricula, but as a powerful symbolic system that reflects and is reflected in everyday life. In short, we view popular culture as one thread in a larger multicultural environment. We also see it as an essential tool in efforts to challenge the Hogwarts' motto in another way, this time understanding the dragon in question as the myriad of students disenfranchised and "left sleeping" by the constraints of the current educational

system. "Tickling" in this case would lead to reinvigorating education by finding ways to make school more relevant to diverse groups
of students. Such a challenge presents great potential for the use of
popular works such as the *Potter* series.

Multiculturalism and the Wizarding World

Before digging deeper into how and why popular culture can be used
in culturally relevant teaching, the idea of "multiculturalism" warrants some unpacking. We use this term in full awareness of Antonia
Darder's discussion of biculturalism, the idea that all students of
color live bicultural or dual lives as they strive to function in both
their home cultural environment and that of the school (structured
to function based on white, middle-class norms).[7] As the *Teaching
Harry Potter* teachers and all their students are people of color, they
negotiate this bicultural experience daily in their respective roles at
school. When we speak of multicultural classrooms, then, we are
speaking of the setting and participants.

Alongside their teachers, students work to negotiate their cultural
orientations and practices in order to find success in classrooms
throughout the United States. The tensions inherent in this process,
given that traditional school dynamics of power and status lie with
the institution, not the family or community, make navigating this
space treacherous for many students who find their native or home
cultures devalued unless a critical, culturally relevant pedagogy is in
place. The teachers here, who navigate their own bi/multicultural
lives, work to practice this form of pedagogy in order to create safe,
contributive spaces for their students. This ongoing experience of
negotiation and diversity creates a setting that is multicultural both
racially and in daily practice.

At first blush, the *Harry Potter* series might seem wholly inappropriate for use in multicultural classrooms. After all, on the surface,
Harry's story bears remarkable resemblance to traditional British
school stories. The central character is a white boy who attends an
elite school, excels at sports, and seeks heterosexual romance. These
and other elements of the story can be read as indicators of the

intended or desired audience for the series—readers who resemble Harry. Despite the centrality of themes such as racism, classism, and genocide within the *Potter* books, and although the series includes several characters of color, racial politics specific to the Wizarding world is privileged over the realities of race and ethnicity in the contemporary nonmagical world.

As media scholar Gizelle Liza Anatol notes in an essay on racial representation in *Harry Potter*, "the inclusion of people of color does not mean the inclusion of any representation of ethnic difference and cultural practices."[8] Using students Cho Chang and Parvati Patil as examples, she notes the superficial treatment of ethnicity, remarking that "Parvati's and Cho's ethnicities are evident in their names, but *only* in their names."[9] We do not know what it means to be Asian in the British Wizarding world, for example. In Chapter 4, Andrew will describe his first discussion about *Harry Potter* with his African American high-school students who described the books as "for white kids." Taking a surface-level reading of the books, their assessment does not seem that far off the mark.

Despite the "whiteness" of the *Potter* books, the series (and, indeed, the entire franchise) exhibits three features that make it not only appropriate but also extremely valuable as a resource in multicultural classrooms. First, as described in Chapter 2, is Harry's status as a newcomer to the Wizarding world. Upon enrolling at Hogwarts, Harry encounters, likely for the first time, a culture that is different from what he experienced living in the suburbs with the Dursleys. Among other things, he must adapt to using different language, new styles of dress, eating exotic foods, and using different technology (i.e., magic—a topic that we will discuss in more depth in Chapter 5). This idea of being a newcomer to a culture or community is likely to resonate with many students, regardless of their specific cultural background. Sandra's story provides one example of the power that this message held for her students; in our discussions with other teachers from across the country, similar stories dominated the conversation.

A second feature of the series that supports a multicultural position is the normalization of difference within the Wizarding world. By creating a world in which every character has features that mark him or her as exceptional—magical ability for one, but also physical features such as a lightning bolt scar, color-changing hair, or a signature scowl—being different becomes the norm. The normalization of difference is not only a fun twist on the traditional boarding school novel but also essential to the overarching messages of acceptance present in the books. In Chapter 6, Allegra sheds additional light on the value of this for her students, who not only bring diverse cultural backgrounds to the experience of schooling but also are marked as "different" due to their placement in special education. For her students, observing a world in which everyone is exceptional—and accepted for their exceptionality—was an important and empowering experience.

The third feature, and one of the series' most important strengths, is the opportunity that it presents for multiple interpretations. Readers do not have to accept the straightforward reading of the text; the size, depth, and complexity of the world and the narrative offer numerous occasions for multiple and competing interpretations. It is in this flexibility that the series becomes not only appropriate but also extremely valuable as a resource in multicultural classrooms. In each of the teachers' narratives, we see examples of adaptable, culturally specific readings of the same *Potter* book. Much as described in reader response activities, the meaning of what is read "... unfold[s] as a reader draws upon personal knowledge and experience to guide developing understanding of the text..."[10] *Harry Potter* can be read using numerous lenses, which is likely why the books have become so successful. This polysemy—multiple meanings derived from the work—is also seen in fans' practices, such as those we describe in Chapter 7.

The teachers' stories presented in this book are special not only because the teachers expertly employ culturally relevant teaching in multicultural classrooms but because they manage to meaningfully incorporate popular culture into that practice as well. These unique, creative teachers demonstrate our shared conviction that popular media should be understood as much more than a simple accessory to schooling. It can serve as more than a simple reward for good behavior, a way to kill time before vacation, or an emergency lesson plan for a substitute teacher. Media and popular culture, thoughtfully and creatively integrated into classroom culture and activities, can provide powerful opportunities for learning through shared experiences, for developing one's critical analysis of media messages, and for relating classroom experiences to the real world.

From Hogwarts to Homeroom: Popular Culture in Schools

As most teachers (and students) will agree, fostering student engagement is half the battle of teaching and learning. The *Teaching Harry Potter* case study teachers, as well as others with whom we have spoken about their teaching practice, emphasize the strength of popular culture—and the *Harry Potter* series in particular—in facilitating student engagement. These teachers found that popular culture was useful not only for hooking students with interesting activities but also for making connections to high-level concepts, and maintaining student engagement over an extended period of time.

The multicultural lens through which we view contemporary schooling acknowledges the ways in which cultural artifacts—including popular media—are also used in shaping aspects of student identity. For example, popular culture has been described as the symbolic "currency" through which youth exchange information about how they see themselves (as a "jock" or "nerd," for example) and jockey for position within social groups. As a tool for engaging students in the classroom, then, popular culture can serve as an enormously valuable resource. Through capitalizing on the investment students already have in particular games, Internet sites, or shows, as well as on the (often encyclopedic) knowledge that they have accumulated about favorite characters (consider *Pokemon*), music, celebrities, and so on, teachers can use popular culture as part of the students' "funds of knowledge" or the understanding and expertise that they bring with them to the classroom.[11] In this respect, all students contribute and feel welcomed, valued, and understood; their knowledge matters. In turn, the teacher is positioned as a learner as well, an inherent aspect of critical pedagogy. Certainly, this requires a reorientation of "expertise." Students' valued popular culture does not "belong" to the teacher in the same way that the information in a textbook or teacher's guide does. Therefore, when popular media is introduced into the classroom, the students frequently become the experts in the room: an understandably scary prospect for some teachers—but an exciting and motivating prospect for students.

Effectively introducing popular culture to the classroom environment requires shifts in disciplinary and classroom management techniques. Many of these mirror Progressive, student-centered educational environments. For example, they include physical changes in the classroom, such as moving desks to allow for collaborative work, allowing students to talk freely during class rather than focusing on silent, individual assignments or discussions strictly moderated by the teacher, or playing music or other media during work periods. Teachers have to be willing to let go and trust the "controlled chaos" that might ensue. Consider the open conversation during class when Sandra read *Sorcerer's Stone*—and the multiple languages used in those discussions.

Beyond novelty and the potential for student engagement, a particular strength of modern franchises such as the *Harry Potter* series lies in their ability to offer multiple entry points to a story. Students described in this book came to the experience of reading *Harry Potter* with different prior experiences and exposure to the series— for example, some had seen the films or played the video games; others had read excerpts from the books or heard about the series from a friend or family member. Most had seen advertising for the films or licensed products. All these prove valuable, however. For example, in Sandra's case she used the students' familiarity with the first movie to help them contextualize the story, especially regarding unfamiliar terms and locations. As Allegra describes in Chapter 6, she uses the first film to directly engage the students in reading *Sorcerer's Stone* as she challenges them to "investigate" the differences between the two forms.

The complex nature of popular culture such as the *Potter* series can also offer students multiple touchpoints *within* the story; whether drawn in by the series' creative (and often humorous) uses of magic, the ongoing romantic trials and tribulations of main characters, the allure of Quidditch, or by something else altogether, students with wildly different experiences and expectations find footholds in a rich text. Once students are engaged, the series offers rich opportunities to discuss issues of importance in our world—but through the lens of the magical setting of the book. As previously stated, the fantasy or allegory may provide much needed distance for students who are learning to adopt a critical approach to information and their own ways of thinking. As will be seen in Chapter 6, Allegra chooses the *Potter* books for her students for this very reason; it gives them a safe space from which to think about their own challenges as they see them mirrored in Harry's story.

The *Potter* series, then, like other rich popular texts, overlaps with numerous areas of inquiry, thus opening up multiple opportunities for entry to those topics. Given this, higher education departments ranging from English to Theology have pioneered its use in some of the top colleges in the country. Yale, UCLA, Georgetown, Stanford, Swarthmore, and numerous other schools have either integrated the *Potter* books into courses or hold classes based around the novels themselves.[12] Edmund Kern, who teaches the course "Thinking About Harry Potter" at Lawrence University, describes how Rowling's works "offer an exceptionally good example of how historical themes and topics can inform fictional storytelling, even when its setting is contemporary."[13] These college-level courses can provide a valuable model for K-12 teachers considering using the *Potter* books in their classrooms, as they demonstrate that the books do not have to be limited to courses in British or Children's Literature. The series can be (and has been) used to teach everything from mathematics to chemistry ("potions") in K-12 schools, and the possibilities are endless.

Despite our enthusiasm for using popular culture, and particularly the *Harry Potter* series, in the classroom, we acknowledge that the politics of schooling makes it difficult for many teachers to bring such products and experiences into their curriculum, regardless of what UCLA and Stanford believe. Much as Umbridge shut down the experiential aspects of Hogwarts' education, current educational policy makes it difficult for teachers to find any "breathing room" to use nonstandardized curriculum. Furthermore, as Andrew discusses in greater detail in the next chapter, a number of questions remain regarding the relationship between schools and *Harry Potter*: should the series be used in schools? How it might be used, and, to what end? Is *Harry Potter* "academic" enough? Is the series "true" literature? If so, what age groups should read the series? In which classes should they do so? What about those students whose parents do not feel that the books should be read based on religious grounds?

Harry Potter does hold an advantage over other examples of popular culture when it comes to acceptance in schools because it is, at its core, a set of books. Moreover, these books are published in the United States by Scholastic, a company with a long, positive reputation in schools in the United States. In addition, some cultural critics have called attention to the fact that the books also carry markers of status and safety, including being written by a (white, female) British author, as well as the series' reflection of traditional literary elements, including the hero's journey. Given these features, the *Potter* books, despite their commercial nature, are a much more "natural" fit within schools than other popular forms such as video games or popular music. In many ways, the *Harry Potter* series is a hopeful example of changing attitudes toward popular texts in schools. Rather than positioning "the commercial" (popular culture) and "the literary" (traditional canon) in opposition much as Harry and Voldemort, wherein neither may live while the other survives, examples of the *Potter* books being used in meaningful, culturally relevant ways, such as those presented by the teachers included in this book, point to slow, but steady change in attitudes toward popular culture and schooling. The degree to which such changes shall prove effective and long lasting remains to be seen, however.

Questioning the Quick Quotes Quill: Developing Media Literacy

Looking beyond student engagement and motivation, what specifically do students learn by engaging with popular culture? In the previous chapter, Sandra described literacy gains on the part of her students; readers will see similar reports in the stories from Andrew and Allegra. In addition to improving students' reading skills,

popular works as part of culturally relevant pedagogy offer important opportunities for students to practice literary critique, critical
thinking, and media literacy.

The *Potter* series, like many other popular texts, offers copious
opportunities for students to practice literary analysis and critique.
The series' complex narrative draws from various literary traditions,
including classical epics, fairy tales, Gothic romance, mystery/detec-
tive novels, and satire.[14] Read as a whole book—or, in some cases,
a whole series—and with the facilitation of a skilled teacher, *Harry
Potter* provides a much richer literary experience than what students
gain from anthologies offering excerpts of various literary classics.

Perhaps more valuable than straightforward literary analysis are
the opportunities that the *Potter* series offers for drawing connections
to issues of importance in our world. Particularly poignant in this
regard are the many conversations that Harry and his friends have
about the structures of power in the Wizarding world: For example,
why some believe that pure-blood wizards are superior to those with
nonmagical parents, whether house elves should be freed from ser-
vitude, or why out of all magical beings, only wizards are allowed
to carry wands? Similar issues around inequality, politics, and ethics
certainly exist in the nonmagical world; interest in such issues is frequently seen in adolescent students grappling with finding a balance
between rights and responsibilities as they gain independence from
their families. However, these issues can (and should) be discussed
in developmentally appropriate ways with younger students using
the politics of the Wizarding world as a concrete example rather
than as a metaphor.

Consider, for example, Hermione's campaign to improve the living conditions of house elves in *Goblet of Fire*. The Society for the
Protection of Elvish Welfare (SPEW) provides a venue for discussing
issues related to race and labor practices. Both the situation itself
and Hermione's understanding of the house elves' social position are
relatively simplistic, particularly compared with "real-world" examples, such as the politics of sweat shops, sex workers, or child labor.
This pared-down, simplified example can be used as an opportunity
for students to explore what they know and how they feel about
the issue. Young readers can discuss the topic as presented in the

books—Why does Hermione think it is a problem that house elves work for free? Should wizards treat house elves differently?—while older readers can use SPEW as a jumping off point to discuss more complex real-world issues.

Harry's own maturing process through the series provides ample models for investigating social issues according to a developmental trajectory. As Harry grows older and becomes more deeply immersed in the Wizarding world, he acquires more information about its politics and begins to form his own opinions about the rights granted and withheld from different segments of society. Harry's growth in this area is amplified upon Dumbledore's death, as he copes not only with the loss of his mentor but also with the discovery of Dumbledore's checkered past. Through Harry's story, readers see a model for scaffolding critical thinking, exploration of the world, and self-development. Harry's experience of the Wizarding world is, at first, very much constrained by what he learns from his teachers, who guide his information seeking and thinking. As Harry gains experience, however, he becomes capable of critical thinking and problem solving on his own and/or with support from peers such as Hermione. This provides a critical lesson in agency and self-determination.

Not only does this type of analysis allow students the opportunity to reflect upon social issues, it also affords opportunities to think and debate how the media portrays and shapes these issues. Such discussions are integral to students' development of media literacy—a sophisticated way of understanding and talking about media (including, but not limited to, written texts) that takes into account the politics that underlies media messages. Whereas standardized curricula eliminate most opportunities for students to think critically about what they encounter in the classroom (much as in Umbridge's class), media literacy requires that students analyze the images and messages in popular culture. As Andrew details in Chapter 4, his students come to use Harry's character development in their analysis of whether morality is a constant. (They decide it is not.)

Throughout the series, Harry and his friends model increasingly sophisticated media literacy skills—including learning to assess the credibility of information in mainstream magical media such as *The Daily Prophet*. Rita Skeeter, *The Daily Prophet* journalist who uses her animagus form (a beetle) to spy on other wizards, is presented midseries as an embodied example of potential dishonesty in the media. From first sight, Harry knows that Skeeter is not to be trusted—but still needs multiple interactions and time to reflect in order to figure out the exact nature and extent of her dishonesty.

In her essay, "Cruel Heroes and Treacherous Texts," Veronica Shanoes describes one pedagogical function of the *Potter* series as teaching critical reading. Just as Harry and his friends must learn to look closely at the texts that they encounter in order to figure out what is true and what is false, so must we carefully decode the texts that we encounter in our world.[15] Shanoes uses the example of Tom Riddle's diary, through which lies leap off the page and literally try to harm its readers. Another example can be found in *The Tales of Beedle the Bard*, the volume of children's fairy tales that Dumbledore bequeaths to Hermione that eventually becomes the key to solving the mystery of the Deathly Hallows. Deciphering Beedle's tales required close, multiple, careful readings and interpretation of the stories, as well as the gathering of additional information from experts.

Current thinking on media literacy emphasizes the need for educators to approach their practice as an effort to prepare students for future encounters with media of all kinds. This preparatory approach stands in contrast to earlier methods of teaching media literacy, which focused on protecting people from manipulative media messages and emphasized strict limitations on media consumption as well as the extensive filtering of content (especially for children.) Taking a preparatory approach recognizes that contemporary society is saturated with media and therefore it is imperative that students are able to develop the skills to make smart choices about the media they consume, think critically about media in multiple formats (both television and print ads, for example), and to share and respond to it in critical and creative ways. Given the current constraints on teacher time and curriculum, however, many students never acquire these important skills. In the case of the three teachers presented here, Andrew, who works in a charter school, holds the most access to utilizing varied media (movies, music, the Internet, magazines, and books) as he works to develop critical viewpoints in his classroom. Even so, he is still limited by time and access, including the Internet firewall that keeps him from modeling effective—and safe—Internet research skills to his students.

Another version of this preparatory approach can be seen in Harry's story. Although Harry was being prepared to use magic, not media, his teachers regularly engaged him in activities designed to prepare him for what was to come. Many of these emphasized problem solving and decision making, rather than prescribing actions and specific answers. Harry's teachers weighed the pros and cons of granting him access to information that had previously been off limits to students, most often agreeing—however reluctantly—to help him learn what he needed to know and providing him with necessary training in advanced spells and skills such as Occlumency (blocking against mind reading). If "real-world" teachers can take a similar preparatory stance, particularly when considering exposure to media containing excessive violence and sexuality or that promotes problematic racist, sexist, or otherwise bigoted ideologies, they have the potential to help students become more discerning regarding their media choices and thus more prepared for their future lives.

Taking a preparatory stance toward media literacy is a powerful means of waking sleeping dragons—whether we are talking about students themselves or the entrenched ideologies that shape schooling. Teaching media literacy is an acknowledgment of the world as it is, rather than holding on to idealized notions of childhood innocence or the cultural value of certain media. Furthermore, such an approach recognizes that students from a very young age are capable of reading media critically and that guidance and practice are valuable in further developing these specialized analytic skills. However, as important as these skills are, they should not be the only aim of teaching media literacy. The ultimate goal, as with other forms of critical pedagogy, is inspiring action. Ideally, through their thinking on and critique of media messages, students will identify opportunities to question what they view, read, and listen to and then enact positive change on local and global levels.

Platform 9 and 3/4

Incorporating popular culture into classroom instruction can provide a bridge between students' home and school experiences, and contribute to culturally relevant pedagogy as well as the development of media literacy. Although popular media has, in the past, proved an unwelcome guest in many classrooms, this trend appears to be changing, albeit slowly. This is likely due in large part to the concerted efforts of talented, innovative teachers such as Allegra, Andrew, and Sandra. Perhaps the moment is right to begin treating barriers to more authentic teaching in public schools like the barrier at Platform 9 and ¾ that separates the magical and Muggle worlds. Although it may look like a brick wall, one can indeed move through it. All one has to do is concentrate, prepare, and run at it confidently, carrying all your school baggage, of course, and with the right mindset, one you will glide right through.

In thinking about the rationale for using popular culture in the classroom, it is also important to think about crossing the barrier in the opposite direction. What will students bring with them when they leave school and move on to their next adventures—college, the world of work, adult society, and so on? In addition, what about the teachers who remain on the school side? How might they use their experiences teaching media literacy and the value of popular culture with different groups of students as an opportunity for their own growth and development as practitioners? Given the current schooling environment, how might such experiences serve as a means for teachers to reclaim agency and choice? How might teachers and students be recognized for the learning and growth that they have achieved through creative, critical, and contemporary engagements with media and learning?

During the course of conducting our research and completing the writing of this book, we talked with a number of teachers who were using the *Harry Potter* series in their classrooms. Despite being from different parts of the country, different types of schools, and teaching different grades, their stories were often very similar. For one, almost all of the teachers we spoke with felt alone in teaching *Harry Potter* at their school site. Many had to fight with other faculty members, administrators, parents, and students to justify their choices. Despite these challenges, they felt that teaching *Harry Potter* was one of the most valuable things that they had done in the classroom because it helped open a door to student engagement and learning.

As important and inspiring as they are, however, the practitioner accounts in this book do not themselves solve the problem of how to both support and then recognize teachers for creative, culturally relevant teaching with popular culture. Assessing and recognizing the value of such practice within (or, perhaps, despite of) the current emphasis on accountability in educational policy seems a particularly onerous task, but it also seems essential. Given the ever growing presence of consumer culture and the expansion of our online, digital lives (issues we will discuss in greater detail in Chapter 5), students need exposure and training in how to critically utilize and approach contemporary culture. To recount Hermione's words from the *Order of the Phoenix* movie, they need time "to think." For these reasons, incorporating popular culture and media literacy into one's pedagogical techniques is vital and teachers should both receive training in these areas and be allowed to utilize what they learn in their classrooms.

In the next chapter, Andrew shows us how this is possible. He describes his beliefs about the value of popular texts, *Harry Potter* in particular, in both preparing for and taking the Advanced Placement English exam and shows how he puts these into practice with his students, to great effect.

Chapter 4

Harry Potter and the Advanced Placement (AP) Curriculum: Teaching AP English in an Urban Charter High School

Surely any books that will be deemed "classics" must reflect something about the values of the age and society that produce them. They must conjure a real world or one that parallels the real world in intriguing ways. They must use language in a way that calls readers' attention to language itself and to how language reflects culture and cultural values. They must have some roots or branches in familiar forms, genres, or subgenres of literature and folklore and yet not be purely derivative.[1]

The Advanced Placement (AP) English course serves as the primary introduction to "college level English" for many students. The course and the exam that follows also present a standard set of "classic" literary works that is rarely contested, or at least successfully. As Lana Whited states above, however, the qualities in "classic" literature that make them enduring also open a door to the introduction of literature that "reflects" current society. Our second *Teaching Harry Potter* teacher, Andrew, approaches teaching AP English using a similar philosophy.

Andrew worked as an English teacher at an African American–centered charter school in Los Angeles during the time of our work together. (He has since moved to Boston where he continues to teach in a traditional public school.) Charter schools, publicly funded yet varied in curricular focus, management, and operational structure, have taken on a significant presence in Los Angeles, representing several different approaches to education. Some charters, for example, utilize a community focus, whereas others center on a college preparatory curriculum. Some charter schools span the K-12 age spectrum, whereas others focus on particular age groups or grades. While Andrew's charter was college preparatory focused, he was able to drive the curriculum more than either Sandra or Allegra. In this, he incorporated popular culture and media outlets, including YouTube and online resources, in ways that the other two teachers could not.

Andrew is a Latino native of Los Angeles. His colleagues and school administration identify him as a skilled educator, he was tapped by the management of his charter school to serve as a leader at the school site, and he serves as a trainer and model teacher for the alternative certification program from which he graduated. An English major who now teaches English, Andrew also gives weight to the argument regarding the value of high-quality teachers working in their actual discipline and what they can accomplish with urban students of color.[2] The high academic expectations that Andrew holds for his students, as well as his belief that varying types of literature, including popular texts that are not necessarily accepted as "literary canon," are acceptable academic choices serve to create a unique platform from which Andrew and his students worked to tackle both their college preparatory curriculum and the AP English Exam.

His natural inclination to utilize popular culture and media in his teaching, and to question perceived boundaries about who different books and movies "belong to" (e.g., are these books for "white kids" only?), motivates Andrew to challenge his students to tackle subjects and books that they initially dismiss. For example, the "literary canon" is a staple of AP English courses, the books generally read and used to answer the essay questions. These are based in what Deborah Stevenson describes as an "academic curriculum" of works considered significant by literary critics and universities.[3] Duncan-Andrade and Morrell call these "literacies of power" as their western, Anglo base reflects those who dominate positions of power in educational—and political—spaces.[4]

Even when there is free choice on exams and students can use any book of "literary merit" to frame their answer, they are expected to draw from particular books and authors, such as Faulkner, Melville, and Fitzgerald, those generally recognized as classics. Popular books or those written for children, and now, the burgeoning young adult genre, do not make the list, something Andrew readily challenges in his classroom. After all, why should only white and/or suburban kids benefit from *Harry Potter* and other young adult novels that have become so prevalent in university courses? He refuses to accept that books such as *Harry Potter* and goals such as success on AP exams are mutually exclusive. This refusal is acted upon through an ongoing critical dialogue with his students, who eventually assert their own ideas about "valuable" reading and viewing choices into the classroom discourse. Andrew's students engage the same critical skills that he models, and their enactment of critical analysis is one of his primary gauges of student growth and success.

As a teacher of African American students, Andrew also exhibits what Gloria Ladson-Billings terms the "central conceptions" shared by the highly effective teachers in her book *The Dreamkeepers*. These include "identify[ing] with the profession" and viewing "the children in their classroom as learners."[5] These teachers also "worked to create a community of learners instead of idiosyncratic connections with students they favored."[6] Andrew's teaching practice exhibits these characteristics, and they resonate throughout his narrative. Most closely tied to the experiences Andrew describes here, however, is Ladson-Billings's third shared teacher conception:

> …the teachers held conceptions of knowledge that were different from many of their colleagues. For these teachers, knowledge was flexible and contestable. Just because something appeared in a textbook they did not feel obligated to accept it. They were careful to search for the warrants that supported curriculum assertions, and they regularly vetted materials by looking for other ways to substantiate claims. As a consequence they expected students to do the same. They did not want their students to just receive or consume knowledge. They wanted them to be able to produce knowledge, and their demands for success were evident in how they taught.[7]

Andrew argues not for eliminating, but for expanding both the AP and African American reading curriculums in order to enhance his students' ability to offer critical analysis of both areas. He argues—contests—the curriculum with his students, unapologetically modeling the process and then inviting, and challenging, his students to do the same. Eventually, they take on the task themselves. The high expectations that Andrew holds for his students, coupled with his willingness to press the boundaries of what are perceived as the appropriate tools for teaching them, mean that he is constantly rethinking, reframing, and debating these issues with his colleagues and students—as a community enterprise.

Andrew's narrative derives from reflective journaling and interviews based around themes and events detailed in his responses. He focuses primarily on the evolvement and progression of *Harry Potter* discussions and activities during his second and third years of teaching, although he summarizes events from his first year to establish the context for ongoing discourse and references other continuing class activities. Andrew focuses on two issues with using *Harry Potter* in his classes: the perceived cultural mismatch between his African American students and books about a white, British schoolboy and the perception (by the school administration and AP teachers in general) of the *Potter* books as children's literature and thus inappropriate to an AP class.

Andrew holds more curricular freedom than Sandra, given the fact that he teaches in a charter school. He does not have to use a scripted curriculum, and as long as he is teaching to the state standards and can clearly show this, and as long as his students' test performance remains high, he is allowed a great deal more curricular leeway than Sandra or, as we shall see in Chapter 6, Allegra. However, the perception issues that Andrew faces run deep and are not to be taken lightly. His training and education as an English major at a rigorous university, however, help give him a breadth of knowledge regarding the "literary canon" including expertise in various ways to approach and thus counter challenges to his curricular choices. This broad familiarity with the field allows for a particular confidence in engaging alternative, creative, and critical pathways to engagement for students. It is vital to note that this teacher characteristic is less present in urban school faculties, where teachers often teach out of their field, yet it is a characteristic that research has linked to student success.[8]

Andrew's account also shows that when prepared appropriately, popular culture and media can be effectively linked to state standards and utilized to garner wider student participation in classroom discourse. In addition, carefully selected young adult literature can be approached critically and utilized as a bridge to access the literary canon, higher-order expression and analysis of the larger society and world. We begin here with Andrew's description of his school and the setting for his *Teaching Harry Potter* story:

There are three pieces of information one should know about our school in order to better understand my account. The first is that it is a charter school with a very small student body. The total enrollment is less than four hundred students and it is rare that a teacher will have more than twenty-five students in a classroom at a time. Also, the school is limited to two floors in one building plus an additional few classrooms on the grounds. As a result, the atmosphere on campus is very intimate. Most of the students have, in some way or another, met all of the teachers. The opposite applies, as there are some students that every teacher knows by name (for good reasons or bad). As a result of this intimate setting, the student–teacher and student–student relationships on campus are very different from a large public school. We know more about each other and spend more time with each other beyond established classroom time.

The second key piece of information is that teachers play an increased role on campus. Because of the school's small size, we also serve as guidance counselors, administrators, security, substitute teachers, and office staff. This omnipresence on campus, key to the logistics of the school running smoothly, gives teachers a heightened awareness of the students' needs and personalities, but also provides the teachers with more opportunities to be viewed as "villains." It was a struggle maintaining my image as a caring teacher and mentor while also carrying out additional duties that required me to separate myself from those roles. For example, one day a low-performing student would receive endless praise from me for doing really well in class, but then I would have to report him to the office because I caught him in the hallway later in the day while on duty.

I was very upfront with my students. I tried to be clear that I had duties as a teacher and duties as a staff member, and they should learn to separate the two. My first year was a constant struggle as students brought outside disciplinary or logistical roles I played into my classroom in a negative way, interfering with their ability to see me as a teacher. I cannot say I actively worked to solve the issue. Eventually, the intensity of the struggle wore off. In my second and third years at the school, the student body and staff grew in number, so I had fewer duties. I relied primarily on my reputation as a teacher to get by during the more intense scenarios. I was the "popular teacher" who cracked jokes, used media in the classroom, and engaged in real-world conversations about gangs, social class, and race relations. That helped to give me credibility with the students.

The last key piece of information is that the school is one of the very few high schools left in Los Angeles that is predominantly African American. Aside from the two district high schools, our charter high schools are the only ones that serve the surrounding African American communities. Our nearly 95% African American student body holds a heightened awareness of uniquely American media and popular culture. This is key because our students are more aware of what is "popular" (such as *Harry Potter*) than students from immigrant families with limited English fluency who may have limited access to cultural trends.

For example, the issue of *Harry Potter* "being for white kids" came up the very first week of school. We were having conversations about experiences during the summer, and one student brought up how she saw a story on the news about the premiere of the fifth film (*Harry Potter and the Order of the Phoenix*). The other students seemed to share her view—that those children (in line) "were crazy" and it didn't make sense to get so excited about a film. I then initiated a discussion about *Harry Potter* and focused the topic more on the novels, which one of the kids labeled as "for white kids." I let the discussion take its course, as it was the first real "conversation" I had with my students in my first year of teaching. Talking together helped me learn much about them and what the experience of teaching this group would be like. I also saw that their values and exposure to popular culture were very different from my own and what I grew up with, which was a combination of mainstream, white American culture and a uniquely Chicano experience. My parents both valued education and literacy and although they were raised in poverty, my father eventually became a doctor. My home was always filled with books and my earliest childhood memories are of my parents reading to me. When I was a little boy, I did not have a favorite movie or TV show—I had favorite books.

My students' argument, though, surprised me. During my college career, I had been fascinated with issues surrounding the social relevance and literary merit of the *Potter* novels, constantly arguing with my professors that they were valuable pieces of literature with analytical complexity hidden beneath a "children's" story. I had never thought, however, about who is exposed to the series and their worth in different demographics. I debriefed with this particular group of students about what made the books "for white kids," and the arguments centered on the dominance of white characters in the films and the lack of availability of the novels to them because the area of Los Angeles in which they live has very few bookstores that sell mainstream, popular fiction. The level of detachment still surprised me, particularly given the coverage of the *Order of the Phoenix* movie release. But the media outlets they listen to did not focus on this event and overall were not spaces that talked about texts and book-related events.

I initially intended on using the books somehow, perhaps as unfamiliar texts on a quiz or as sample passages for instruction. But this conversation made me want to reveal to my students what I saw as the validity of the works (novels and films) as important pieces of world (literary) culture. I decided to use the novels and associated media outlets to see how my students would react to the stories and characters and also gauge how those reactions differed from my own and those of other fans. This is the point where I began to develop the lesson plan using the films to teach the *Bildungsroman* (coming of age) genre.

Teaching Harry

The reactions of Andrew's students to *Harry Potter* illuminate perceived boundaries about "ownership" that not only include school and reading (those books are not for "us") but also cross boundaries of everyday life and popular culture. The "hidden curriculum" of their schooling experience, those things that are not learned explicitly through the established curriculum, the "unintended outcomes of the schooling process"[9] (e.g., social practices, power structures, and expected roles around gender, race, and socioeconomic status), indicates or teaches students about that which is "appropriate" for them. The hidden curriculum also reaches out into their everyday choices about the media outlets and activities in which they decide to take part. Advertising supports these messages. Needless to say, what students also find available in terms of consumer choice reinforces these decisions, as is evident in the students' explanation to Andrew about their lack of access to books.

Interestingly, Andrew's narrative mixes two different views of legitimacy regarding the *Potter* novels and popular culture in general. On the one hand, popular culture is not considered legitimate enough to be located within advanced educational spaces or "the canon" (reserved for privileged students). As Michael Apple states, "Anything 'popular,' anything from that sea, is 'soiled.' It is 'not quite serious knowledge... It is not quite real.' "[10] Therefore, popular texts should remain pleasure reading for the masses, not required reading in advanced English courses. Yet *Harry Potter*, perceived and marketed as "for white kids" in this context, is not available casually either. Andrew's students do not initially read or engage *Harry Potter* books or media on their own (with one exception, as we shall see) and therefore do not then participate in either the academic or social (formal and informal) experiences around the book. These are not natural boundaries, as is evidenced by the teachers here who describe their students' active engagement with the text. Once exposed, the students engage the story, some deeply. This is evident in each *Teaching Harry Potter* teachers' account. In addition, the fact of *Harry Potter's* worldwide acceptance across cultures and languages attests not only to the power of savvy marketing but also to its multicultural accessibility. The boundaries perceived by Andrew's students, then, are socially constructed (unnatural) and reinforced in both local media outlets and schooling structures.

This is tricky space, no doubt. Not every student will love or relate to *Harry Potter* or books like it, but that should be a choice made from experience. Those experiences should include reading literature from different genres and diverse authors. Here it is important to reiterate that the need for a diversity of representation in school and school curriculum is vital. Lisa Delpit states:

> When instruction is stripped of children's cultural legacies, then they are forced to believe that the world and all the good things in it were created by others. This leaves students further alienated from the school and its instructional goals, and more likely to view themselves as inadequate.[11]

Books such as *Harry Potter* should not take the place of a book by an African American author in Andrew's curriculum and they do not. However, he does make the *Potter* series available—and accessible—helping to broaden the scope of his students' critical, cultural lenses. The opportunity is provided to engage in critical conversations and to reap the benefits of thinking through these with a teacher who holds expertise. In their work with urban high-school students, Duncan-Andrade and Morrell describe their efforts to facilitate "...a healthy dialogic space and the completion of superior academic work."[12] Andrew's class reflects similar goals.

Certainly, Andrew's background and personal experience with literacy and literature motivates his determination to share what is essentially a form of empowerment with his students: critical reading and thinking skills. To engage his students in this manner, however, he first needed to cross boundaries around differences in race, status (teacher/disciplinarian versus students), and power to gain his students' trust:

On the first day of school in my first year of teaching, one of my African American students walked into my classroom, said "I already had Spanish," and walked out. It was a quick reality check telling me that, for the first time in my life, my racial identity was going to be at the forefront of many conversations. That first year, all of my students except one were African American and many of them had never before encountered a Latino person who could speak fluent, academically oriented, accent-free English. The African American community, for me, was the racial demographic with whom I had the least experience. I attended a mostly white and Asian school system, had mostly white and Asian friends in college, and am part of a large Mexican family composed mostly of immigrants and first-generation Americans. During the first few months, my students made many flat-out racist statements, without even realizing the severity of their mindsets or thought processes. Questions such as "Why can't they just learn English?" and "Why do they always ride with so many people in one car?" were not only shocking but also completely offensive to me. I took advantage of those teachable moments, however, and addressed the issue head on, often stopping in the middle of a lesson for the sake of what I felt was a more important discussion.

After many mistakes, and in some instances being accused of racism by students and parents alike, I found a method that worked. When my students made blanket generalizations about a group of people (usually the Latino community), I tried to equate it with a stereotype often associated with African American culture. A joke about burritos or tacos turned into a discussion about the perception of African Americans and fried chicken. Questions about the inability (or perceived unwillingness) of Latinos to learn to speak English were answered with questions about the role of Ebonics in African American communication. Students began to respond to this method. In a city torn by a race war, I pushed my students to think not about the differences between my own community and theirs, but the similarities.

The minority experience in America, and particularly Los Angeles, is truly unique, but the similarities in the experiences of Latino and African American youth became a common topic in my classroom. The method I used was extreme and, to be honest, I'm not sure if a white teacher could have executed it without an outrageous response. While trying to avoid the development of an "us versus them" mentality (the "us" being black and Latino Americans and the "them" being white Americans), I encouraged my students to see the power in promoting the common achievement of ALL minority youth. We educated each other on the difficulties of our minority experiences as well. I recall a field trip to a local amusement park for "Physics Day." One of my students, as an experiment, asked me to walk into a gift shop full of white students from one of the most prestigious local private schools. I did so, and then uneventfully, walked out. When my student did the same, I watched as all of the white students saw him and immediately walked out of the gift shop. While I encouraged my students to celebrate the commonalities of African American and Latino Americans, they made sure I understood the struggles that were uniquely African American.

I extended this method into my instruction around *Harry Potter*, particularly after my students dismissed it as a novel "for white kids" and indicated that the characters' race immediately eliminated the novel's appeal for them. In addition to the use of media, I focused on character struggles that were similar to those of my students. I particularly focused on the first novel, since there we learn about the factors that make Harry, Hermione, and Ron different (and thus, immediate friends). Harry lives with adults who are not his parents and who mistreat him terribly. Ron comes from a family experiencing economic strain, forcing him to wear hand-me-down robes for which he is tormented. Hermione comes from an entirely different world and is not accepted by some because her parents are Muggles (something purely biological and beyond her control). It was through these character attributes that I was able to direct my students to look beyond race. Instead, we focused on what made these three characters part of an "other," a term we began to use in our discussions about race in general. Harry, Ron, and Hermione were no longer "white" characters; they were just characters.

Andrew's ability to engender trust and thus engage his students in such powerful self-reflection allow for extraordinary teachable moments in his classroom. Much as Sandra, Andrew also holds a set of gatekeeper keys that he uses to open the door to complex, critical learning experiences. While these keys are initially challenging to use, Andrew is eventually able to engage them readily. As a result, much as the other books in his class, we see how *Harry Potter* becomes something his students relate to and own; the books and movies become theirs and they use them to scaffold their understanding of other perspectives and texts. Through this process, his students grow their confidence enough to eloquently reflect back on themselves as well as challenge the construction of the AP English Exam itself. In short, they become discerning readers, critical thinkers and learners who are willing to share their ideas with others.

Professionally, Andrew believes that his students should have access to *Harry Potter* and other forms of popular culture in a manner that provides the means, opportunity, and motivation to engage these works on both fronts: the academic and the everyday. He readily discusses how young adult literature is utilized to scaffold learning toward more canonical, as well as culturally relevant, forms. In this respect, he creates a new meeting space where culturally representative text clash, mix, and blend:

Introducing the *Harry Potter* novels into my classroom required two important tasks. I had to invest/engage my students in a group of novels they clearly had dismissed as irrelevant and uninteresting. I also had to find a way to justify the books' presence in a classroom at a school that prides itself on building a college-ready and rigorous environment. I realized the books' label as children's novels would raise some eyebrows when I used them in the classroom. Therefore, I decided to begin with the films as an introduction to the literary elements of the *Bildungsroman* (coming of age) genre of literary fiction. I commonly use films to teach major thematic, character, and plot concepts to struggling readers; however, my AP students (all of whom read and write above grade level) have also used the combination of *Harry Potter* novels and films to engage in logical debates that permit them to apply their skills to real-world issues. For me, this indicates the level to which the *Harry Potter* series and its accompanying media can work together to help make student knowledge more lucid to the student and teacher.

I work to hook the students on texts. For example, there was strong resistance to *The Great Gatsby* in the beginning. He's a rich, white guy, and the book is hard to read. I did prereading activities where I made *Gatsby* into a soap opera and the students were engaged and got really excited about the story. I've found that if they don't feel the text is something interesting or relatable, they disengage. So with *Potter*, I started with the films; if I had started with the books, I think the students would have resisted.

In preparation, I made sure the lesson connections to the California Content Standards were posted and obvious in case an observer walked into the classroom. I selected clips from the first and second films that focused on Harry and his development between the two movies. I showed two scenes from the first film, *Harry Potter and the Sorcerer's Stone.* The first was the scene in the girl's bathroom, when Harry and Ron battle the troll using the most basic magic they know. The second clip was the final "battle" scene of the movie featuring Harry and Professor Quirrell. I also showed clips from the second and fourth films. The first, from *Chamber of Secrets*, featured the three main characters using Polyjuice Potion [which temporarily transforms their appearance] to investigate their suspicions about Draco Malfoy. The second clip, from the fourth movie, *Harry Potter and the Goblet of Fire,* was the battle scene between Voldemort and Harry at the film's end. Through the progression of these clips, my students saw Harry and the other students advance their knowledge of magic as well as how they used it. The students also noticed that Harry's bravery level increased, from the once inexperienced, frightened boy to someone now engaging in a duel with a powerful wizard.

Students then engaged in a Socratic discussion mapping out the differences they saw in Harry's character, using the limited information available from the film clips. The discussion focused on determining character traits from character actions/words (one California standard) and using the information to construct what they thought was an element of the genre (another standard). The lesson went very smoothly and students performed well on the summative assessment testing those standards. Their success on these assessments then gave me some leeway with the administration in terms of using the novels more in class.

I came to also use the *Harry Potter* collection to build students' abilities to make text-to-self and text-to-world connections with literature from outside their cultural point of reference. Together, we explored the reasons they attached the "*Harry Potter* is for white kids" stigma to the series while I also used the books as a reference point to introduce ideas the students would encounter later in the curriculum. Because *Harry Potter* is more readily accessible, some students are able to develop a clearer understanding of complex literary ideas and then use their new understanding to make broader connections with and analyze canonical texts. Issues of character maturation, ambiguous morality, epic heroism, betrayal, and social conformity are only some of the more complex literary issues I've introduced using *Harry Potter*.

I also began using scenes excerpted from the novels, changing the names of characters, as unfamiliar texts for students to read and analyze through prepared questions on assessments and worksheets. These questions were similar to essay prompts and California Standards Test (CST) questions, but focused on scenes from the *Potter* novels. At times, I would let students know, after the fact, that these passages came from the novels. Their reactions were mixed. Some students were pleasantly surprised and laughed at themselves for becoming interested in a passage from a book they once dismissed. They also asked questions about the characters and the larger context of the passage. However, I did not answer these questions. Instead, I directed them to the classroom library, where there sat copies of the books. Because I usually picked scenes at the height of conflicts or emotional struggles, students became very interested in reading the books. I began to see the novels pop up more and more during independent reading periods. More students also began to watch the films at home.

One of the more interesting comments during discussions about the novel was "Mr. V, you can't even tell that the characters are white when you're reading." It appears as though the marketing of the books and the target audiences of the films are what created assumptions about them. My main question for my students in this situation was, if they could not tell the race of the character in the reading, why did the depiction of white characters in the film trailers turn them off to the books? The students talked about how the immediate appearance of white characters suggests they will not be able to relate to the book, despite never having read the plot. While students admitted the wrongness of such ideas after engaging with the novels, it was an important talking point for the class. How many experiences had my students missed out on simply because they assumed they would not be able to relate to (and thereby not enjoy) the experience? And, what role do teachers play in creating a connection between students' cultural experiences and the world around them? I found the same issue coming up when I played music in class during work time. If an alternative rock or pop-rock (my music of choice) song came on, I received comments about my taste for "white people music."

At my school, there is also constant pressure to read selections students "can relate to" meaning African American literature, and we do that as well. But I am also a firm believer in the literary canon and its modern relevance. Pike tells teachers that "indeterminacy" is key to understanding texts—a culture clash between the author and readers' worlds resulting in a better understanding of a text's broader meaning.[13] *Harry Potter* provides students with a springboard to engage with texts through this type of "clash" because it makes complex literary devices more lucid for students. Some of my students even analyze the series itself in a manner that makes its relevance equal to any selection from the canon. When African American students can read a work filled with characters, settings, and conflicts completely removed from their own experience, they still have the ability to think critically about it and apply it to their own world through familiar tensions between differing cultural experiences.

One key breakthrough highlights the use of *Harry Potter* in the learning process in my classroom. "Student A" was a special education student who had an Individualized Education Program (IEP), and struggled with an auditory processing disorder. She was, however, an adamant fan of video games. During the first lesson, when I used clips from the *Harry Potter* films, she demonstrated knowledge of the plot of the fourth book. In fact, she was able to contextualize the clips for many of the students around her. As it turned out, she owned and often played the video game for the fourth film/book, resulting in her knowledge of the novel's events. The lesson served as a hook for her, and her class participation and achievement levels increased after that, especially once she and I began having daily, informal conversations about the books. It was not long before she read the entire series and started writing her own fan fiction (where she made up her own stories about the *Harry Potter* characters). She shared some of her stories with me and they were very creative. In one story, Harry crash-lands on his broomstick and it's his first year so he doesn't know where he is, but he uses the little he does know to help himself. In this student's case, the key point for me was the multitude of media attached to the *Harry Potter* series. Watching a student become involved with the novels through other media forms was eye opening; it's clearly a useful strategy for teachers in the classroom. If I can also teach my AP Literature class the complexities of moral development through showing one of the *Harry Potter* films and then having a debrief discussion about it, why not do so?

Challenging the AP Canon

Andrew's use of *Harry Potter* and related media in his AP class forced him to face issues not only of relevance (to his students' lives) but also of perception. Both popular and labeled children's books, *Harry Potter* faces an uphill battle in terms of acceptance into traditional, canonically based courses, regardless of the books' growing presence in colleges and universities. Andrew is not alone in considering this issue. The popularity of the *Potter* novels has spurred a great deal of debate regarding the validity of *Harry Potter* as a work of "literary merit." This particular debate remains ongoing among literary critics and AP graders alike and is likely to continue rather than diminish as a passing trend. As mentioned in the previous chapter, the number of university courses centered around, or including, *Harry Potter* only continues to grow. In addition, the young adult genre is experiencing an exciting period of growth, spurred in many ways by J. K. Rowling's success. Daniels states that,

> ...the difference today lies in the burgeoning attitude of respectability the YA literature is receiving in the present day, thanks in no small

measure to the success of J.K. Rowling...It seems that *Harry Potter* has opened up a whole new arena of respectable scholarly debate.[14]

Given that students raised on *Potter* who found that it opened the door to other books and media forms have become college students and teachers themselves, and if logic follows, will, in turn, soon become literary critics and exam designers as well, one wonders what the future holds for the place of *Harry Potter* and other contemporary works of young adult literature in classrooms.

*   *   *

While a great deal of this debate is taking place on college campuses, it is increasing in secondary schools as well, although not necessarily through a friendly discourse. Public schools are traditional institutions, slow to change in any fundamental manner. After all, the basic structures of classrooms, schedules, required courses, and so on remain familiar over generations. As the teachers here attest, curricular innovation is one of the most difficult areas to pursue. Curriculum is also a highly contested space, driven by external political mandates (from the right and left), traditional expectations of what "history" or "science" or "literature" should entail, and today, standardized testing content.[15] In AP courses, which are geared toward passing a specific exam, the testing content, based in university-level expectations for students, drives the curriculum. Ironically, while universities have historically influenced secondary curriculum and school structures,[16] their more alternative practices, using popular texts to anchor courses, for example, do not transfer the same way. Andrew then finds himself addressing the issue of *Harry Potter's* relevance on the one hand and explaining to his students why they might not want to use it as an example on the actual exam on the other hand.

The growing presence of young adult literature does provide some context for Andrew's discussion. Granted, not all books are of the same quality, but that is true of all literary forms and provides further opportunity for critical analysis of popular text as well as discussions about choice in reading. Most of these books, Suzanne Collins' *The Hunger Games* series,[17] for example, are accompanied by a range of affiliated media including movies, games, TV shows, and websites, which support their presence. Readers discuss the stories on discussion boards, comment on authors' blogs, live blog and chat online, track author appearances, listen to and create podcasts, and write and share their own fan fiction based on the characters. Do these activities add to the view of young adult literature as "unworthy of serious literary evaluation" or, in the long term, will they serve to help the genre "break through?" Regarding *Harry Potter*, Wallace and Pugh argue that,

> ... as myriad *Potter* Web sites and fan fiction sites illustrate, readers of these books expend considerable energy debating plots, speculating about what will happen in the final installment, and revising the stories by writing their own versions...
>
> Harnessing such interest and energy in the service of teaching close-reading skills and critical thinking requires that we pose engaging questions that draw students into the issues motivating critical theory. To that end, we offer examples of how the *Potter* texts can engage students in studying constructions of cultural values in relation to consumerism and social class, gender inequity, homophobia and heteronormativity, and racial tokenism.[18]

Such exercises certainly require the facile use of higher-level, critical thinking skills. Obviously, many young readers are already engaging these in online spaces, so the content and platform are viable. The question remains as to whether this will translate to more traditional spaces. Andrew is clear and direct about *Harry Potter* on this front: it is complex and relatable and provides helpful scaffolding for his students as they practice the higher-level analytical/interpretive skills required to pass the AP English Exam.

> The Advanced Placement English Literature and Composition Exam requires students to write three essays in the second portion. One of these essays is an open-ended prompt that asks students to apply a broad, general concept of literary analysis to a novel or play of their choice. In addition to listing novels or plays that would be ideal for the prompt, the exam also states that students may select a "novel or play of literary merit" not provided on the list.
>
> I was initially reluctant to involve the *Potter* novels in my AP Literature class because they are still not commonly accepted as "works of literary merit." When I attended the Southern California

AP Institute in the summer of 2008, one of our major debates centered on whether or not the novels were acceptable topics for open-ended writing prompts. The central issue stemmed from the idea that despite their relatively easy reading level, the novels have the potential to encourage deep analysis and critical thinking. Some teachers were unable, however, to get past the "simple" plots and reading levels. The argument did not make any sense to me, especially since many books that have been used on the AP Exams have a relatively low reading level. I brought up examples of low-level, high-analytical content books including *The Giver, Ender's Game,* and *The House on Mango Street.* All of these books have been listed as options to use in completing open-ended essay prompts. I argued that while all of them were "easy" to read in terms of fluency and comprehension, they lend themselves to the deep level of analysis required on the AP Exam. Even though *The Giver* is a sixth-grade reading book, can a student in sixth grade analyze the complex message behind the destruction of a Utopian society in the mind of a child? Can a seventh grader truly grasp the message behind the children of *Ender's Game* being used as a militia through playing a video game? Can they address the commentary the novel provides on the rapid development of technology? I posed these questions to the group and was met with mixed reactions. While some teachers were open about being convinced, others continued to suggest that the *Harry Potter* series did not lend itself to deep, analytical assertions because of the "simplicity" of its content.

While the issue remained undecided among teachers at the Institute, one of my students proved the novels hold true analytical potential. During a practice writing session, an AP prompt I gave my students asked them to analyze how any major literary character encountering a moral dilemma contributed to that particular work's meaning. One student who had been struggling in the course wrote an excellent essay about how Harry's constant need to break Hogwarts' rules, despite the inherent "wrongness" of doing so, was necessary for a virtuous outcome. She suggested that the issue revealed the work's message that morality itself does not function in a straight line, meaning morality is not constant, but relative. She ended her essay with a brief comment about Voldemort and how he grew to use the same abilities that Harry possesses but for evil, again proving that morality is not a constant. This student's ability to successfully write her essay increased her level of confidence in the class. She realized she was indeed capable of analyzing literature at the expected level, and that she had instead been struggling with comprehending the assigned texts. As a result, she became more dedicated to her reading once she understood the specific obstacle preventing her from analyzing at an AP level.

Eventually, she improved her grade in the course from a low D to a solid C. Although she did not pass the AP Exam, her score of 2 indicated that she had clearly made major gains during the school year. She is now in her senior year, currently earning a high C in her English class, and has already been accepted to several California State University campuses. This is truly a remarkable improvement, given that when I first began teaching her in English 10 in fall 2007, she was writing at a sixth-grade level and her analytical skills were quite low.

Practice AP prompts are common in my classroom, as the skill of writing under pressure is essential for success on the exam and my students need help developing this over the course of the year. My unit exams focus on a specific novel or play and always contain an open-ended essay prompt directly from a past exam, thus allowing students to demonstrate their knowledge of a literary work in addition to the skills of writing a timed, open-ended AP exam prompt. After we read Toni Morrison's *The Bluest Eye*, for example, I used a prompt from the 1995 AP Literature Exam that centered on alienated characters, asking them to "Choose a play or novel in which such a character plays a significant role and show how the character's alienation reveals the surrounding society's assumptions or moral values."

As is common practice when I return graded open-ended essays, the class brainstormed other works that would have also sufficed to answer the prompt. One student, an avid reader, asked about the possibility of writing about the *Harry Potter* series and focusing on Harry as an alienated character. I responded that I was not sure if the work was considered one of "literary merit," and described the debate I took part in at the 2008 Southern California AP Conference. I told them this same conversation topic came up and pointed out that the session leader, an experienced AP Literature teacher and exam grader, did not feel *Harry Potter* was an appropriate AP work. I also shared the fact that I personally disagreed with her.

As a means of both measuring this student's skills and genuinely wanting to hear her perspective, I asked her to explain more specifically how she would have addressed the prompt. In very precise detail, indicating her thorough knowledge of the novels as well as her skills with literary analysis, the student discussed Harry Potter's alienation due to his social class. She defined his social class as very complex, having financial stability while also not being brought up in upper-class Wizarding society and traditions like other wealthy characters, such as Draco Malfoy. Harry's social status as "isolated," she said, was highlighted by his befriending of Ron (a relatively poor character) and Hermione (a character with "Muggle" parents). She felt Harry had been drawn to these characters, who held their own clear points of social isolation, because of his own. The student's definition of isolation, framed by her understanding of the function of character past and foils, was a clear demonstration of the skills necessary to pass the exam.

At this point, another student jumped into the conversation. Although he admitted to never having read any of the books, he had seen all the films and used the information from the films to continue the conversation. Harry, he argued, as a character who continuously breaks rules and laws in order to carry out what the viewer (reader) sees as the most moral actions demonstrates the flawed emphasis on tradition in the Wizarding world. Another student who was well versed in the films added that had Harry not experienced his social alienation (along with Ron and Hermione), he may have been less likely to defy rules in order to do what he thought was "the right thing." These two students addressed the second point of the prompt, analyzing Harry's character to expose the Wizarding world's weaker moral choice in always emphasizing tradition.

After this very strong analysis of the plot and characters, other students began to question why the work was not considered one of "literary merit" and challenged the idea that works of "literary merit" even had to serve as the focus point of the AP Exam. One student's quote, in particular, stands vividly in my mind: "If we show that we can analyze a piece of literature at the college level with all the skills we learned in the class, does it really matter what book we choose? Literature is so subjective. It does not make any sense for someone to judge whether or not a book has merit." Another student added, "It's hypocritical. They want us to find value where someone reading without a critical eye would not, but they do the same by blowing off books like *Harry Potter*."

The conversation continued with students justifying other popular works of literature, including the *Twilight* series. While I personally do not feel the *Twilight* novels possess the same complexity in theme and character development as the *Harry Potter* series, the fact that many of my students (again some familiar with the novels and others familiar with the films) were able to engage in an enlightened debate that demonstrated mastery of the skills was truly inspiring. I wonder how the AP graders and exam authors would fare against my students in a debate about the *Harry Potter* series.

In Andrew's classroom, the students' use of the *Harry Potter* books crosses borders of race, class, and culture. Simultaneously, they hold such constructions up to a light in order to dig deep in their analysis of the value and place of the work in their lives. Andrew's critical pedagogy and culturally relevant approach, which both questions and adapts the curriculum to meet the students' needs and perspectives, allows for a classroom where the agency of the students enables them to make and remake the text for themselves. Andrew's growing awareness and use of media and technology in his class also opens the door for students to construct their own versions of the story and consider how these can be used to create both new and old magic.

Another Take on Teaching *Harry Potter*: Writing the Potterverse

Each spring, my school has a one-week "mini-term" during which regular classes are suspended, and students take a single weeklong seminar on a subject that is not a part of the regular school curriculum. Three times, I've offered fanfiction writing workshops. Two of them were specifically geared toward *Harry Potter*. The third time, students could write in any fandom, and about three fifths of them chose the Potterverse.

The basic premise of the workshop is that the core of good fanfic (and good fiction in general) is authentic conflict that stems from deep, textured understanding of character. Students pick a central character for their fic and then, using exercises adapted from Heather Lattimer's *Thinking Through Genre*,[19] flesh out their understanding of that character. From there, the students create a central conflict for their character and begin to flesh out a story. The rest of the week is spent writing and workshopping drafts with the rest of the class. Student response to these workshops has been very positive. The majority of them have been fanfic readers but not writers, and in their end-of-course reflections, they said they appreciated the scaffolded process used in the class as a way to help them get their own stories up and running.

I chose *Harry Potter* for two reasons. First, on a purely personal level, *Harry Potter* fanfic was what I was writing at the time. Second, even though the series wasn't yet complete (the first time I held the seminar, *Half Blood Prince* was the most recent book), it was clear to me that *Harry Potter* was a generational text for these students. They had grown up with it, in many ways going through school as Harry did. I conducted a highly unscientific nonrandom focus group study (read: I asked students in my classes) if they thought there would be interest in a fanfiction writing workshop, and the answer was a resounding YES. I later found out that one of our Humanities/Lit teachers was also a *Harry Potter* fan (though not really into fandom), and she provided some much-needed professional expertise in the original workshop design.

Dave
Mathematics teacher, Chair and Dean, private independent high school, San Francisco, 22 years experience.

Chapter 5

Old Magic, New Technologies

"Your sons flew that car to Harry's house and back last night!" shouted Mrs. Weasley. *"What have you got to say about that, eh?"*
"Did you really?" said Mr. Weasley eagerly. *"Did it go alright? I—I mean,"* he faltered as sparks flew from Mrs. Weasley's eyes, *"that—that was very wrong, boys—very wrong indeed..."*[1]

Despite the series' setting in the 1990s, one hallmark of a Hogwarts education is its lack of modern instructional tools and techniques. Students prepare written school work with quills on parchment scrolls; in his sixth-year Potions class (the magical equivalent of chemistry), Harry borrows a textbook previously owned by one of his father's classmates and uses the annotations scribbled in its margins to complete his class assignments, which had not been updated or changed in the interim years. Even Hermione's beloved library appears to be quite outdated, lacking an electronic catalog and the multimedia that are a growing part of school and public library holdings.

Teachers at Hogwarts do not project overheads or PowerPoint slides; they do not use online resources to enhance their lesson plans; and they do not use e-mail to communicate with their students' parents. (Indeed, parent–teacher contact seems to be minimal, aside from parents receiving students' test scores by mail.) Likewise, students have no exposure to the digital media or electronic devices familiar to most readers of the series. There is nary a computer, cell phone, gaming system, or MP3 player to be found at Hogwarts. In fact, in *Goblet of Fire*, readers learn that Muggle electronics, were they to be brought onto Hogwarts grounds, would be rendered inoperable by the magical protections that have been placed on the school.

This absence of technology extends beyond Hogwarts to the entire Wizarding world. Margaret J. Oakes has described the Wizarding world as "high-tech/low-tech": a "contradictory combination of advancements worthy of the most far-reaching science fiction, and an everyday life so antiquated as to be medieval."[2] As we have also discussed in earlier chapters of this book, a similar situation can be observed in classrooms across the United States, in which the realities of the contemporary world frequently clash with "medieval" systems for teaching, discipline, and social life normalized in schools. In terms of technology, this conflict can be seen in the outdated or inoperable hardware that fills computer labs (especially those in poor, urban districts), in policies that prevent students from using available technologies in schools, including policies that ban mobile phones and Internet filtering software, and in activities that "tack on" technology in superfluous ways to existing lessons. The differences between a learning environment in which learners can access and use technology in meaningful, creative, and extended ways and an environment in which technology is treated as an afterthought or an obstacle are glaring.

Although technology is but one element implicated in this tension between the "real" world and the world of school, its contributions are significant on both practical and symbolic levels. As part of the day-to-day operations of schools, technology can be a gateway to resources that might otherwise be inaccessible; it can provide alternative means of expression and participation for students with disabilities; and it can be an integral part of institutional systems and communication practices that support the success of teachers and students alike.

Symbolically, the presence (and absence) of technology in schools calls attention to the fact that the world is changing; there is more information in the world, more competition for students' attention, and less time to learn everything needed to participate in a dynamic (and unstable) society. Despite the stranglehold of standardized curriculums, many schools and teachers are under increasing pressure to prepare students with technology skills that they are expected to need for future work and civic/social participation. The absence of technology in many schools, then, not only indicates the students' exclusion from technology-enhanced learning experiences in the present but also symbolizes their potential exclusion from potentially important modes of participation in the future.

*   *   *

Although digital media and technology do not appear at Hogwarts in forms that are familiar to contemporary readers, there is a pervasive technology throughout the Wizarding world: magic. Following Raymond Williams's definition of technology as a "systematic treatment" of a form of "practical arts,"[3] the magic used in the Wizarding world and taught at Hogwarts certainly counts as a technology. Magic provides all of the necessary tools for everyday life, from domestic chores such as cooking and cleaning to leisure activities. Magic is also used for more sophisticated needs such as defense, medical care, transportation, recording and storing information, and, of course, teaching and learning. In the words of literacy researcher Peter Applebaum, magic is "ironically a technique for solving all of the problems that technology and science have always failed to solve."[4]

At Hogwarts, magic is embedded within the experience of schooling. It is the topic of instruction across the curriculum as well as a primary medium for participation in classes. For example, teachers use magic to present information to students as well as to facilitate experiments and simulations. With the notable exception of the changes enacted under Professor Umbridge's rule, much of the students' time in class is spent using magic—for example, practicing spells, brewing potions, reading tea leaves, and caring for magical creatures. Furthermore, because magic is a "practical art," the magic taught and practiced in school is directly linked to that which students already know and use outside of school and/or will need in their future adult lives.

Magic is not used at Hogwarts in the superficial ways common to technology use in U.S. schools: it is never used as a reward for finishing "real" work or good behavior; it is never used to automate drills or to otherwise substitute for thoughtful instruction. Magic is central to the design of the curriculum at Hogwarts; it is not added on to existing lesson plans to make them more "fun," nor is it restricted to classes for gifted students. To be fair, magic does not come with many of the barriers that schools face with technology. None of the Hogwarts teachers have to apply for grants to obtain magic; there is not a "magic lab" for which teachers compete for access, nor is there an understaffed "magical maintenance" department responsible for keeping magic up and running for the entire school. Furthermore, magic is not treated as a commodity in the same way technology is in our world. Although the shops in Diagon Alley and Knockturn Alley sell magical objects and supplies, there is no planned magical obsolescence (at least during the timeframe we observe in the series), nor competition between magical brands. Magic is at once the focus of instruction and an invisible technological system shaping the culture and practices of the school.

As an all-encompassing technology, there appears to be little space in the Wizarding world for magical innovation. Magic has a long history and is generally used according to established customs and moral codes. Magical innovations are typically presented as history (e.g., Dumbledore's discovery of the 12 uses of dragon's blood), silly tricks for fun and profit (e.g., Weasley's Wizard Wheezes), or dangerous perversions of magical law (e.g., Voldemort's creation of multiple Horcruxes). As the excerpt that opens this chapter illustrates, however, these divisions are not always black and white, even in the minds of adult wizards such as Arthur Weasley. His response to Harry and Ron stealing his flying Ford Anglia—wonder and excitement rather than the disapproval expected (and demonstrated) by his wife—demonstrates that not all wizards are satisfied with the lack of magical innovation in the Wizarding world. Indeed, some of Harry's greatest accomplishments in the series are encouraging other wizards to open their eyes to the possibilities of change and helping to teach others how to distinguish between positive and harmful examples of magical innovation. In this way, Harry once again stands as a powerful model for educators looking for ways to enact change and progress in schools.

If, as we have throughout this book, we look to the *Potter* series as a commentary on contemporary education, we find a useful model for embedding technology into the everyday lives of schools. However, given the need for operational and curricular change in schools, we also see in *Potter* a cautionary tale about ignoring calls for innovation. Like teachers, technology is an unequally distributed resource in our schools. We must pay attention to the causes and outcomes of unequal access to technology and the modes of cultural, civic, and educational participation that it enables, as well as to the unique needs of teachers in using technology for culturally relevant teaching. Moreover, educators must be involved with technological innovation.

This chapter considers gaps in participation with technology— disconnects between home and school uses and between imagined ideals and actual uses—that affect both students and teachers. In this examination, we look closely at the ways in which the *Teaching Harry Potter* teachers used digital media and technology in their classrooms to introduce new skills and modes of participation to their students. The chapter asks questions about technological and curricular innovation, considering the potential of initiatives such as Science, Technology, Engineering, and Math (STEM) education, New Media Literacies (NML), and 21st Century Skills for supporting authentic learning with technology in all schools and for all students.

The Participation Gap and Other Dark Magic

Whereas magic is embedded in the social fabric of the Wizarding world, technology remains a disruptive force in our world. Technological progress and innovation constantly result in new information, new ways of accomplishing tasks, and new questions about how and why we live the way we do. At the same time, technology highlights and exacerbates social inequalities, not only making visible the differences between technological "haves" and "have nots" but also raising the stakes of such inequalities. Both the disruptive nature of technology and its impact on social inequalities are especially obvious in educational settings.[5]

In describing technology as "disruptive," we do not mean to characterize it negatively. Indeed, disruption is necessary for innovation and progress. In the educational world, this disruptive force is often portrayed in terms of potential for improving a stagnant educational system. For example, *The New York Times'* recent Education Issue was completely dedicated to educational technology and provided glowing reviews of a number of initiatives to improve teaching and learning with technology. Looking at innovative hardware, software, and online platforms such as online tutoring, e-readers, and mobile phones, the *Times* issue spoke to the growing belief that, in their words, "technology is redefining what it means to be a student—or a teacher."[6]

The history of educational technology points to its repeated positioning as a "magic bullet" for fixing various problems, including improving student motivation, increasing the rigor of assessments, and streamlining and standardizing instruction. Educational historian Larry Cuban traces the link between instructional technology and school reform in the United States beginning in the 1980s, driven by "a loosely tied national coalition of public officials, corporate executives, policymakers and parents"[7] with three shared goals: Improving productivity and efficiency of schools; supporting active and relevant teaching and learning; and preparing students for participation in a rapidly changing workforce. While these goals seem like reasonable, positive expectations for educational technology, additional expectations—for example, that technology will fix deep, longstanding problems related to inequality—have become problematically enmeshed with them.

State and federal educational technology initiatives to date have focused on providing access to computers and the Internet in school computer labs and classrooms. These efforts to "wire" schools have been successful in providing basic access to hardware and connectivity. A recent report from the U.S. Department of Education claims that, as of 2008, every public school in the country has one or more computers with Internet access available for instructional use and 97% of schools had one or more computers with Internet access located in classrooms and designated for instructional use.[8] According to this report, the national ratio of students to instructional computers is 3:1. If we think carefully about the baseline of the claims made here—that every school in the country has *one* computer available for student and teacher use, and that *almost* every school has *one* computer in *most* classrooms—calling many of our schools "wired" hardly seems appropriate. The 3:1 ratio can be interpreted as further evidence of vastly unequal distribution of technological resources when we take into consideration the (slowly) growing popularity of one-to-one computing, most frequently made possible in affluent districts or by philanthropic efforts of high-tech firms. For every school that has a 1:1 ratio, how many must have much higher ratios to arrive at the 3:1 average?

At the same time that schools have limped along in their efforts to integrate technology, personal technologies have become ever more ingrained into the rhythms of everyday life for most Americans. For example, personal technologies that allow people to work and play anywhere, such as laptops, mobile phones, and MP3 players, have become ubiquitous. Digital media formats have extended the scope and reach of entertainment and information, while Web 2.0 applications have changed (and challenged) the ways many people establish and maintain social relationships and participate in community and civic life. Youth have been active participants in adopting new technologies and modes of participation.[9] Given the speed with which contemporary technological innovation is happening and the scope of the changes in which it is involved, the disconnected, "magic bullet" approach to technology taken by many schools appears to be more problematic all the time.

Educational technology is much more fragmented and contested than either magic at Hogwarts or the magical qualities ascribed to it by technologists. The technology students (and teachers) use at school rarely resembles that which they use at home; what is used in either locale usually differs from what has been identified as "ideal" for educational purposes. This "participation gap" is a result of physical access to technology—the old concerns of the digital divide—as well as access to knowledge and ways of participating with new media and technology. Put simply, the difference is between simply wiring schools for Internet access and providing students with the access and the skills that they need to use the Internet in productive ways, including new modes of civic and cultural participation. Current thinking about the participation gap pushes beyond simple equations for access to consider the sociocultural factors and implications of learning with and about technology.

Most research on the participation gap to date has focused on situations in which the digital media and technology students use outside of schools is superior to that which they access at school. These investigations are primarily concerned with the effects that losing access to participatory learning opportunities while at school might have on student motivation, comprehension, and literacy development. To this end, a number of recommendations for ways to incorporate the technologies of youths' everyday lives—video games, learning toys, mobile phones, and social network sites, for example—into the classroom, either as part of teacher-driven instruction or as resources for self-directed learning, have been made by teachers, researchers, administrators, and others interested in education.[10]

Issues around the participation gap are another reminder of the importance of critical pedagogy and culturally relevant teaching. As with popular culture more generally, using digital media and technology in the classroom requires a shift away from the notion of the teacher as the only expert in the room—an idea that is directly related to critical pedagogy's calls for "decentering" teachers and flattening the hierarchies in place in classrooms. Considering the needs of a local school community is also essential to addressing inequalities in participation. Unfortunately, many of the efforts that schools and districts have made in implementing technology have ignored the specifics of students' and teachers' needs, instead enacting a "one size fits all" approach to technology.

As with many other changes to educational policy and curriculum, teachers frequently have been left out of this conversation, despite being a strong source of information and ideas about how to best use technology to teach in their particular classrooms and school communities. This leads us to another gap in participation—the differences between the technological resources and training that teachers receive and what they need to use technology in expert, culturally relevant ways in multicultural classrooms. For example, Andrew, who generally experienced greater freedom in relation to curriculum and pedagogical style, ran into a technological roadblock when trying to use online videos in his instruction—the school's firewall, which blocked many useful sites in the name of protecting students and the school's network from malicious content. Even though Andrew had an idea and a plan for a project that was exciting and salient to his students, he could not implement it using the resources available at school. He, like many other teachers, found it necessary to supplement the school's technology with his own, for example, by downloading videos or other media materials at home and bringing them to school in offline formats.

This type of "teacher participation gap," whereby teachers struggle to balance their needs for engaging and culturally relevant pedagogy with restrictions on access to technology, consists of challenges at the individual, school, and systemic levels, including the following:

- Teachers are not consistently trained to use technology in their classrooms; neither teacher preparation programs nor current professional development models provide the breadth or depth of training required for teachers to develop the skills needed to use technology in meaningful ways in instruction.
- Teachers may be encouraged to use digital media in their classrooms, but are not provided with the necessary technology or technical support to do so.
- Teachers are not empowered to use technology in culturally relevant ways.
- Teachers are required to enforce rules about students' technology use—for example, restrictions on music players or cell phones on campus—regardless of the teachers' personal beliefs about the technology.
- Teachers are subject to totalizing school/district policies regarding technology, such as the installation of web filtering software or the adoption of a standardized curriculum that requires particular technology use; teachers are thereby restricted from

making decisions about the media/technology that is most appropriate or useful for their students.

- Teachers are not consistently encouraged to innovate their teaching using digital media, nor are they recognized or rewarded for using technology in successful, creative ways in their classrooms.
- Teachers do not have opportunities to discuss technology with colleagues or other experts.

As this list demonstrates, there are significant disconnects between expectations for teachers' uses of technology and the realities of classroom technology use. Although recent research indicates that more teachers are incorporating digital media into instruction than ever before, there is little consistency in the frequency of digital media use or in the instructional methods employed by teachers.[11] Access to computers, audio/visual equipment, and other technology (such as smart boards or mobile tools) remains highly variable within and between schools. This lack of continuity and strategy is, understandably, a source of frustration for teachers and educational technology advocates alike.

Similar issues of access and participation can be seen within the Harry Potter series with regard to magical ability. For example, early on in *Harry Potter and the Sorcerer's Stone,* readers learn that Hagrid, despite being a teacher at Hogwarts, does not have a wand. He carries a pink umbrella that he uses occasionally to cast spells—but only when necessary, and often to unexpected outcomes. As he tells Harry:

> "I'm—er—not supposed ter do magic, strictly speaking. I was allowed ter do a bit ter follow yeh an' get yer letters to yeh an' stuff—one o' the reasons I was so keen ter take on the job—" [said Hagrid.]
> "Why aren't you supposed to do magic?" Asked Harry.
> "Oh, well—I was at Hogwarts meself but I—er—got expelled, ter tell yeh the truth. In me third year. They snapped me wand in half an' everything. But Dumbledore let me stay on as gamekeeper. Great man, Dumbledore."[12]

Although Hagrid clearly was an expert in his subject area (Care of Magical Creatures) and a passionate, caring teacher, one has to wonder how Dumbledore justified keeping a teacher on staff who had such minimal preparation and experience with magic and who was, in fact, not allowed to do magic without express permission (presumably from Dumbledore himself.) Hagrid, armed with only a pink, flowery umbrella,[13] was destined to face difficulties in his job—he did not have the training or tools to carry it off properly.

In thinking about the participation gaps faced by our teachers and students, our goal should be twofold: first, to replace the "pink umbrellas" that stand in for appropriate, functional, and relevant technology. In so doing, care must be taken to undo the damage of being marked as less expert with technology and less welcome to take part in new, technologically mediated modes of civic and cultural participation. Second, to question the reasons behind such gaps: why *was* Hagrid teaching without the tools that other faculty members (and Wizards in general) took for granted? Why are so many teachers in our schools left in similar positions? Key to achieving both of these goals is fostering innovation, not just in hardware and software, but also in curriculum and school culture. Taken together, these innovations could fundamentally change the way technology is used in school, leading to more embedded, engaging, and culturally relevant practices.

Does the Room of Requirement Have WiFi? Innovation in Education

Although the Wizarding world struggles with innovation throughout the Potter series, Hogwarts is fortunate to have (somewhere) within its walls a lab that knows no limits in providing for innovation: the Room of Requirement. Known for its ability to provide the user with whatever he or she needs at the moment the room is found, one particularly important example of this magically magnanimous space supporting innovation can be seen in its use by Dumbledore's Army (the DA) in *Order of the Phoenix*. We have discussed the DA at length in Chapter 1; however, it warrants a brief re-examination specifically in relation to technology and innovation.

The Room of Requirement provided the DA with a space in which to meet outside of the purview of formal instruction in order to experiment with technology (in this case, magic). Much of the work of the DA was based on simulation—students simulated attacks on one another in order to practice defensive spells. Some of these spells (such as the spell to conjure a *Patronus*) require deep commitment to the simulation, as students needed to imagine their happiest memory in order to activate the spell. The stakes for failure in the DA meetings were very low—primarily social (e.g., potential for teasing by peers) or emotional (e.g., frustration). The pedagogical space provided by the Room of Requirement was a low-risk environment that allowed students to practice magical skills outside of formal assessment systems and without fear of failure. This setting was ideal for fostering innovation and authentic learning.

Let us consider for a moment what the Room of Requirement might look like in contemporary (nonmagical) schools. Some might imagine the cavernous space filled floor to ceiling with computers and other technological gadgets; we, on the other hand, believe that the Room of Requirement would *not* resemble the computer labs and technology depots that are becoming more and more familiar in schools. What the Room of Requirement would have, in our imaginations, is wireless Internet access (WiFi), mobile devices (such as smart phones), digital media production equipment, and support and space for students to experiment with these new tools. What these technologies share is that they are transformative; particularly for young people, each of these technologies has changed approaches to information access, interpersonal communication, and personal expression. Combined with the support of family members, teachers, and/or peers and opportunities for play and experimentation, these technologies can be particularly transformative in education.

Reliable WiFi is an excellent example of technology that mirrors the embeddedness of magic. WiFi is always present (or at least most of the time), can be used with multiple devices, can be shared among multiple users without a great deal of coordination or compromise, and also facilitates and encourages sharing information and media. Mobile phones have opened up spaces for communication and participation; currently undertheorized as a tool for critical education, educational applications of mobile phones represent an area of potential growth during the near future. Similarly, digital media production tools are potentially transformative tools, as they facilitate students' abilities to create media that talks back to problematic ideological messages and to communicate with a community that extends beyond the walls of the classroom. All three of these technologies—WiFi, mobile phones, and digital media production tools—can contribute heartily to the creation of a participatory space in which students can come to own the learning that goes on within it.

Since none of the schools in our world have a Room of Requirement (or, at least, not one that's been found) to facilitate access to transformative technologies, curricular innovations seem like the next best place to look for transformative and embedded approaches to technology. In the next section, we review three initiatives that demonstrate innovative approaches to curriculum and in which we see great promise for enacting an embedded, systematic approach to educational technology that resembles the place of magic in the Wizarding world.

Imagining Magical Futures: STEM Education, 21st Century Skills, and NML

The need for innovation in curriculum, school policies, pedagogical techniques, and educational technology has been recognized by diverse stakeholders within education—from high-tech research and development firms to local and national educational policy makers. Currently, three initiatives—STEM education, 21st Century Skills, and NML—offer promising models for curricular innovation. We examine each in turn.

The first, STEM education, is currently a high priority in national educational policy. A September 2010 report released by the President's Council of Advisors on Science and Technology[14] highlights the importance of STEM education to the current and future health of the United States, noting that "STEM education will determine whether the United States will remain a leader among nations and whether we will be able to solve immense challenges in such areas as energy, health, environmental protection, and national security"[15] by producing workers for global economy, cultivating scientists and encouraging innovation, and improving literacy. According to the report, STEM education will "strengthen our democracy by preparing all citizens to make informed choices in an increasingly technological world."[16] Efforts to encourage participation and improve teacher preparation in STEM fields have emerged in the forms of technological tools, including video games and mobile applications, grant competitions, extended learning programs, and professional development opportunities. Technology and digital media are central to efforts in the STEM fields, both in terms of tools and skills directly related to engagement in the fields themselves and in defining, delivering, and promoting innovative products and opportunities.

The second area of emphasis is 21st Century Skills—a set of competencies across three domains: life and career; learning and innovation; and information, media, and technology. 21st Century Skills incorporate many of the critical approaches to literature and media that we have discussed in previous chapters, updating them to take into account the needs of learners in an increasingly technology-driven, networked, and global world. Like STEM education initiatives, 21st Century Skills connect directly to concerns about students' preparation for future participation in a global economy and society. "The competitiveness and wealth of corporations and countries is completely dependent on having a well-educated workforce…"[17] In a recent editorial in the *Huffington Post*, educational policy experts Esther Wojcicki and Michael Levine commented on the need for schools to focus on the global aspects of 21st Century Skills by improving availability and quality of foreign language programs and introducing global issues—from history and economics to health—across the curriculum, by adding benchmarks for global competencies to current assessment schema, and by facilitating increased opportunities for students' investigations of other cultures via technology. As Wojcicki and Levine write, educators need to "propel US schools out of their time warp while taking advantage of young people's natural interests in other nations' people, culture, music and technology."[18]

Closely related to 21st Century Skills (and particularly to the information, media, and technology branch of 21st Century Skills) is the idea of New Media Literacies (NML). NML share some characteristics of alphabetic literacy: at a basic level, they are ways of "reading" and "writing" texts. They also share characteristics of critical media literacy, in which the ideological underpinnings of media are exposed and examined. What is different is the definition of "text," which is expanded to include all types of digital media, as well as the understanding of literacy as a set of processes that are fundamentally social, as opposed to a set of cognitive skills that an individual has or lacks.[19]

Instead of viewing new media as replacing existing media (read: books), most NML researchers and supporters view new media in terms of additional layers of literacy. This view of literacy is a challenge to traditional ways of valuing media—with books at the top and electronic media such as television or video games at the bottom. For many teachers, this is a substantial shift in thinking and an uncomfortable adjustment. In an interview to the *Frontline* documentary *Digital Nation: Life on the Virtual Frontier*, Henry Jenkins described teachers as "preachers of the book," noting that teachers "defended the book against mass culture; and now they're defending the book against the web. And they've not been taught to conceptualize that we can have books and computers too. That we can enhance how we teach reading by engaging the broader community through the Internet." He highlights the lack of training and discussion about new media for teachers as a "central struggle" for justifying NML in school settings.[20]

A common thread among STEM education, 21st Century Skills, and NML is an emphasis on incorporating content and new pedagogical approaches across curricular areas and learning environments. Indeed, one of the strengths of new technologies is in expanding opportunities for learning outside of the classroom. Places that have not before been considered legitimate sites in education—online spaces, video games, children's books—are re-imagined as powerful locales for teaching and learning.

Support for STEM education, 21st Century Skills, and NML has come from both the private and public sectors. In particular, high-tech firms have a stake in defining expectations for future workers—as well as an interest in students as current and future consumers of their products. As David Buckingham notes, the discourse of technical skill joins together "education, the commercial market, and the future worker/consumer."[21] This point is not to be taken lightly. In their involvement in defining competencies and supporting activities, technology companies and charitable organizations become "sponsors of literacy," which Deborah Brandt describes as "any agents, local or distant, concrete or abstract who enable, support, teach, model, as well as recruit, regulate, suppress, or withhold literacy—and gain advantage by it in some way."[22]

Interestingly, conversations around STEM education, 21st Century Skills, and NML are, by and large, taking place separately from discussions about literature. There are benefits and dangers in framing these three initiatives as technological at the expense of connections to traditional literacies and content. Benefits include attention from government and powerful scientific and high-tech companies, all of which are concerned about cultivating skilled scientists and manufacturers for future employment. This attention leads to funding, which can lead to better facilities and materials for instruction, as well as continuing training and professional development for teachers. The danger in focusing on science and technology to the exclusion of literature (and arts/humanities in general) is missed opportunities for connections across disciplines and the deep understanding of the world that can come from multidisciplinary perspectives. Another danger is that the potential for innovative and creative uses of technology within the humanities will be undervalued, resulting in financial support and public attention being funneled away from these disciplines, leaving them unable to continue to innovate and meet students' educational needs.

The *Teaching Harry Potter* teachers have varying levels of experience, training, and support for teaching with technology. Andrew and Allegra, both in their mid-twenties, share with their students the experience of growing up in a media- and technology-rich world. Although they each come from different cultural and ethnic backgrounds, grew up in different families, and attended different schools, both teachers are part of a generation that many describe as "born digital,"[23] in which media and technology are normal parts of everyday communication, entertainment, learning, and work. In this way, Allegra and Andrew possess the advantage of shared experience in understanding and connecting with their students about and through technology. Whereas more senior teachers such as Sandra may be familiar with media and technology and may be highly supportive of and skilled in its use, they did not grow up in the same media and technology climate and, therefore, have to catch up with their students, possibly even changing the way that they think about technology.

To return to our magical analogy, we can see a similar difference between Harry, who comes to the magical world with no knowledge of Wizarding culture, customs, rules, and so on, and Ron, who grew up in a family and a community for whom magic is the dominant culture. Through his upbringing and earlier experiences in the Wizarding world, Ron knows the history, heritage, and social norms of the world and therefore approaches the world very differently than does Harry. As Rowling is quick to point out, however, this does not imbue Ron with superior magical abilities, but with a different orientation to magic and the magical world. The third member of "the trio," Hermione, is a further reminder that culture is not destiny. Hermione is Muggle-born, a novice in the Wizarding world like Harry. However, Hermione's academic strengths (and, in particular, her curious nature and voracious reading habits) help her compensate for lack of early experiences with magic, contributing to her success at Hogwarts and beyond and helping her earn her reputation as "the cleverest witch of [her] age."[24]

Three practices in particular should be highlighted as strengths of the case study teachers' use of media and technology in the classroom. First, the teachers were open to multimedia as a way to access the books and as channels for extending the classroom reading experience. Second, each teacher addressed issues related to the participation gap. Third, the teachers selectively used technology to support student learning.

Although the *Potter* series has a large, worldwide readership, it would be a mistake to assume that all students are familiar with the books. In fact, although many of the students in Sandra, Allegra, and Andrew's classes knew of *Harry Potter*, the teachers each reported that most students were familiar with the characters and stories because they had viewed the films and/or played the video games; very few students in any of the classes had read any of the books before our teachers introduced them. For some teachers, particularly those who subscribe to traditional notions of literary canon and divisions between high and mass culture, the fact that students did not come to the series through the books might be disappointing. However, these teachers felt differently; as each of them noted during the course of our work together, the various entry points by which students accessed the series (e.g., films, video games, or other products) contributed to student engagement and, in some cases, provided opportunities for critical discussions that might not otherwise have happened. For example, in each teacher's class, students initiated and participated in discussions about differences between the films and the books, questioning and critiquing the choices made in the adaptations.

The teachers' willingness to incorporate students' prior experiences with *Potter* products, combined with their *Potter*-related in-school uses of media and technology, resulted in classrooms where literature was viewed as more than dusty old books. As in the *Harry Potter* books themselves, where diaries come to life, newspaper photos move, and children's stories are more than what they seem, the books took on new lives as interactive objects in our teachers' classrooms. Although the full experience of *Harry Potter* as a transmedia franchise (meaning that parts of the story are told across different media) may not have been possible in the case study teachers' classrooms, the ways in which the books and related media were valued, discussed, debated, and represented in student work reflects the teachers' and students' facility with 21st Century Skills/NML, as student work and classroom discussion took advantage of porous boundaries between media and demonstrated many of the critical skills associated with these two initiatives.

As we have discussed in earlier chapters of this book, the choice to use popular culture in the classroom is, particularly at this moment in educational history, a subversive and often risky choice for teachers to make. Adding technology to the mix can raise the stakes even further. However, each of the case study teachers noted the importance of introducing the books to the students despite the potential backlash from other teachers, administrators, parents, or students themselves. In this way, the teachers were addressing the participation gap head on. Refusing to accept the idea that their students would miss out on reading at least part of the series that has been declared a global phenomenon of popular culture and that they themselves found rich, meaningful, and enjoyable, our teachers made the accommodations necessary for their students to be able to experience the books.

Furthermore, each teacher strived to help his or her students make connections between the books and the prescribed school curricula—for example, by using the books to practice for Advanced Placement exams or reading along with an audio book in an effort to improve reading fluency. For these efforts, the teachers selectively leveraged technology to support student learning. For example, as we will discuss in greater detail in the next chapter, Allegra used an audio book version of *Harry Potter and the Sorcerer's Stone* to support her special education students' developing reading abilities. She chose to use the audio books based on her assessment of her students' needs, her understanding of what would improve student engagement with the text, and the reality of the technology that she had available to her in her classroom. Teachers having the freedom and expertise to make this kind of assessment of their students' needs and interests is an essential step toward producing an embedded approach to media and technology in schools.

Pedagogical Polyjuice Potion

Throughout the *Potter* series, we see various characters use Polyjuice Potion to conceal their identities. In *Chamber of Secrets*, Harry and Ron use the potion to disguise themselves as members of Slytherin house; in *Goblet of Fire*, Barty Crouch, Jr., passes as Mad Eye Moody by sipping Polyjuice from his hip flask; and in *Deathly Hallows*, six of Harry's friends magically take on his appearance with the potion in an attempt to facilitate Harry's final departure from Privet Drive. In each of these scenarios, magic creates the appearance of change, but does not fundamentally change the person taking Polyjuice; the way she or he behaves is not affected by the potion; she or he remains in full control of his or her thoughts or actions. Once the potion wears off, the wizard who ingested it returns to his or her normal form with no residual effects.

It is an unfortunate reality that many of the attempts to incorporate digital media and technology into schools resemble the effects of Polyjuice Potion—a masking of one's true identity (in this case, established ways of thinking and teaching). Polyjuice has a temporary effect—as its effects wear off, what is underneath is slowly revealed—and it becomes clear that that which was masked was not actually changed at all. Cole and Kalantzis describe this phenomenon not in terms of magic, but as "[using] new technologies to learn old things in old ways."[25] They go on to describe the disappointing outcomes of such practice, writing:

> We can set up the new media devices in our contemporary world to do old-fashioned didactic teaching...We can use computers to re-create traditional, transmission pedagogies that embody a mimetic relationship to knowledge; absorb the theories, practice the formulae, learn the facts, appreciate the greats of the canon, internalize the socio-moral truths that others have deemed will be good for us...[26]

How often does exactly what Cole and Kalantzis caution us about happen in schools? Have overhead projector slides become PowerPoint slides without any thoughtful changes to the assignment in order to improve interactivity, update the content, or increase opportunities for critical discussion of the topic? Are technological resources such as laptops used to introduce students to a wider range of information or are they so locked down by software and filters that they prevent exploration and experimentation? Have assignments that require media production—such as creating web pages or multimedia presentations—been designed to utilize the unique strengths of those media, or are they the same, tired essays delivered in new packaging? The unfortunate reality is that the answer to all of these questions is, all too often, *yes*.

In order to survive and save the Wizarding world from Voldemort, Harry needs to learn magic that is outside of the normal curriculum at Hogwarts. Similarly, our students need to learn ways of using technology that are new and different from anything that has been taught before. We cannot continue to "Polyjuice" old pedagogy and old technology if we hope to prepare students for the world that they will enter as adults. As we have discussed in this chapter and throughout this book, we see great hope for change in technological and curricular innovation, a commitment to embedding technology in the day-to-day operations of schools according to the specific needs of students and teachers and according to the principles of culturally relevant teaching.

In the next chapter, Allegra describes her experience reading *Harry Potter and the Sorcerer's Stone* with her special education students. Allegra's story demonstrates the value of technological innovation for supporting culturally relevant pedagogy and meaningful uses of technology. As a special education teacher, she faces challenges that are different from those that Sandra and Andrew have described. She and her students struggle to cope with an exceptionally distressed school environment while also trying to catch up to grade level in reading. Within these overdetermined circumstances, Allegra turns to fantasy literature as an opportunity to encourage students to engage with issues of difference as well as to imagine possibilities beyond their everyday experiences.

Chapter 6

Entering the Forbidden Forest: Teaching Fiction and Fantasy in Urban Special Education

Squibs would not be able to attend Hogwarts as students. They are often doomed to a rather sad kind of half-life (yes, you should be feeling sorry for Filch), as their parentage often means that they will be exposed to, if not immersed in, the Wizarding community, but can never truly join it. Sometimes they find a way to fit in... but they still function within the Wizarding world because they have access to certain magical objects and creatures that can help them.[1]

The challenges and privileges of being different are key themes in the *Harry Potter* series. Given this, the fantasy world of *Harry Potter* potentially demonstrates additional appeal to students in special education because of the ways in which the theme of difference is woven into the story. Throughout the series, readers observe a number of characters in their efforts to cope with being exceptional. Harry offers a particularly interesting example, as he is notably different from his family and peers in both the Muggle and Wizarding worlds. His lightning bolt scar is but one mark of his difference; having magical abilities sets him apart in the Muggle world, while certain specific magical skills, such as being able to speak Parseltongue, mark him as having different, and potentially more powerful, magical skills than do other wizards.

While at Hogwarts and in his adventures beyond the school, Harry encounters a number of other students, adults, and magical creatures who, like him, have one or two characteristics that mark them as different from the average wizard. Many of these characteristics are physical: Ron's ginger hair, Hagrid's size, or the skeletal appearance of the Thestrals, for example. Other characters, Luna for example, demonstrate their difference through their behaviors.

The school setting is essential to exploring these themes. Unlike in Muggle schools (in the series and in our world), where pressures to adhere to normative behaviors and established status hierarchies often make it difficult for exceptional students to succeed, every student at Hogwarts is recognized for his or her special abilities; indeed, nonmagical people (Muggles and Squibs) are not allowed to enroll in the school. Despite the physical, psychological, and ethical challenges inherent in wizardry, having the specialized knowledge and abilities needed to practice magic is understood to be a privilege throughout the Wizarding world.

In the nonmagical world, schools also foreground differences in students—though not often in the positive light characteristic of the Wizarding world. Being "special" in Muggle schools does not always result in respect for one's unique abilities and patience for one's challenges. In fact, students deemed "special" or "exceptional" are often cloistered in special education classrooms, separated from the rest of the students and teachers, and invited or allowed to join in the general community only occasionally and in very specific, structured ways. In this way (among others), special education students are marked not only as different but also as deficient in some way. Furthermore, in urban schools such as the one discussed in this chapter, the legacies of racial and class-based inequalities are amplified in special education.

This chapter is coauthored by Allegra, who at the time of our work together was a third-year special education teacher in a large Los Angeles area public middle school (she has since accepted a new position in a charter school in Los Angeles). Her account emphasizes the unique challenges of special education in underperforming urban schools and highlights the creative approaches that she took in creating a meaningful, challenging, multicultural learning environment in her classroom. As a special education teacher in an urban public school, Allegra holds unique perspectives on issues of difference and on the types of literacy resources that best meet the needs of urban students in special education. She has used the *Potter* series to help her students engage with these issues in creative and meaningful ways.

Allegra's reflections address her students' relationships with the larger school community, consider the ways in which issues of difference shape her students' educational experiences, and offer insights into her teaching practice, including her unique approach to sharing *Harry Potter and the Sorcerer's Stone* with her students.

School Context and Background

My school is located in a very economically depressed part of Los Angeles. The area has a long history of poor schools, social unrest, and disconnected family units. Over 90% of our students qualify for the federal free lunch program. We have been a program improvement (PI) school for over ten years. Our stronger students read about two years below grade level and our daily attendance rate fluctuates between 90% and 95%.

The school is surrounded by four different urban housing projects, each associated with a particular gang. Our student population is predominately comprised of children from these housing projects, and given that fighting amongst residents of the various projects is rampant in the surrounding neighborhood, students reenact these conflicts on campus. The campus is socially disjointed and there is an obvious tone of hostility amongst the students.

Very few teachers choose to teach at my school; fewer choose to stay at the school long-term. Teacher retention has always been an issue. The school experiences 30%–50% faculty turnover each year.

Faculty members generally fall into one of three groups: One group has taught at the school for about ten years and has become very complacent with the environment on campus. These teachers have developed the tools needed to run their classes the way they want them and appear indifferent to the context and conflict that surrounds the campus. The second group consists of new teachers assigned to the school through Teach for America or a district or university intern program. New teachers experience various levels of success and stay at the school for about two or three years before transferring to a new school or leaving the teaching profession entirely. The third group is made up of a constant rotation of substitute teachers. Substitutes are vital to the operation of the school as there are five to ten unfilled teaching positions each year. I am a member of the second group. After three years at the school, I will transfer this fall to a local charter school to continue teaching.

My expectations and assumptions about teaching have been deeply challenged during my time at the school. I believed, and still believe, that the ideal teacher is a facilitator that provides tools and a context for students to create meaning out of the material they are presented with. I think this is particularly true of special education teachers. Ultimately, a teacher should push her students to think and form opinions and conclusions of their own, using the course material as a springboard. While I understand the need for standards, I think that it is important to remember that the goal of teaching is not to be able to say that you, as the teacher, covered all of the material, but to say that your students are able to effectively communicate their understanding using each level of Bloom's Taxonomy. What I have found at my school, however, is that the primary goal of a teacher is to control her students. If a teacher is able to control her class, what she actually does with them is a secondary concern.

For example, no one in the administration knew about the *Harry Potter* project. I can only assume that their reaction would have either been indifference or annoyance. I did not really get the sense that any of my advisors were interested in innovative curriculums. The administration valued scripted curriculum, the types that used research-based best practices, because they were interested in raising the school's test scores as soon as possible. They wanted to operate in a world that guaranteed a quick rise in scores, and they were not interested in anything that did not have documented success in that vein.

All the students I teach qualify for special education services under the classification of "Specific Learning Disability." This means that my students have demonstrated prolonged challenges in one or several of the following areas: reading, writing, speaking, learning, or reasoning. My seventh-grade students on average read at a second- or third-grade reading level, have third- or fourth-grade comprehension skills, and struggle with advanced computations, such as multiplication, division, and working with integers. Their conceptual reasoning skills are far below grade level; they struggle with performing higher level thinking skills such as analysis, inference, and synthesis. All of my students have legitimate learning disabilities, but their ability levels are additionally depressed due to understimulation and years of rote instruction. My students possess many isolated skills, but do not know how to use them to form conclusions, make judgments, and manipulate the world around them.

Students end up in special education at my school for a variety of reasons. However, the general rule of thumb that I adopted while I was at [the school] was that Black boys were referred to special education because of their behavior and Latino students were referred for their limited English proficiency. This is not to deny the existence of learning delays in several of the students; however the impetus for referring these students was not their learning barriers, but their non-normative behaviors in class. General education teachers of my generation are given tools to make in-class academic accommodations for students who are struggling—but only to a point. Students who are low readers, nonfluent English speakers, or students with externalized behaviors are still viewed as a disruption to the general education setting. I believe that students in special education pick up on this messaging and internalize these perceptions. They believe that they are in special education either because they are "bad," or because their English language skills are poor. It is not uncommon for students in our special education program to reach middle school without ever engaging in any conversations about learning disabilities or different learning styles. I think this creates a situation in which students, as well as teachers, begin to lose sight of the goal of special education placement, and special education quickly becomes a place where "problem" students go, as opposed to a service that students receive.

The most recent data available from the U.S. Department of Education report that 6.6 million students (ages 3–21) received special education services in 2007–2008. Of these 6.6 million students, 39% (2,574,000) received services for a specific learning disability.[2] Today's special education policies and procedures are the result of a specific historical and political trajectory, the most recent installment of which has been indelibly shaped by the No Child Left Behind (NCLB) Act and standardized testing mandates.[3] Allegra's tenure as a special education teacher has taken place during this most recent policy wave that maintains the basic premises of the Individuals with Disabilities Education Act (IDEA), the most significant of which is that students with disabilities have access to the general curriculum.[4] The NCLB Act protects this assertion and includes special education students in requirements for standardized assessment of Adequate Yearly Progress.[5] Given the testing requirements, much of the instruction in special education (and, indeed, throughout schools) is focused on test preparation.

Despite pressures related to testing, Allegra chose to read *Harry Potter and the Sorcerer's Stone* with her seventh-grade students. As she noted in our discussions, she did this for a number of reasons: to present students with challenging and engaging reading material, to provide opportunities for students to practice sustained, fluent reading, to emphasize the enjoyment that can be found in reading good books, to encourage students to use their imaginations and visualize what they read, to encourage text-to-self connections, and to share with her students a piece of literature that she herself valued and enjoyed reading. As struggling readers, Allegra's students required extra support to work through the difficult text, which she provided through a number of creative pedagogical and technological strategies and tools.

Given the school context, including its status as chronically underperforming based on standardized test scores, as well as her students' placement in special education, Allegra's choice to include her students in activities outside of the prescribed curriculum was a personal and political risk. Schools facing funding cuts due to underperformance have, by and large, turned to highly structured curricula designed to prepare students for standardized testing. Special education students are at even greater risk than general education students for being left out of such activities in favor of additional practice of basic skills. However, Allegra believed that her students deserved a richer experience. Determined, she designed an innovative reading unit utilizing technology as a support.

Reading *Harry Potter* with your Ears

My students were familiar with *Harry Potter* solely through the movies. Not all were immediately excited when I announced that we would be reading the book; however, a few were won over by the challenge to investigate the ways the book [*Harry Potter and the Sorcerer's Stone*] was different from the movie.

Analyzing the difference between a book and its film adaptation was not an uncommon practice in my classroom. On previous occasions, I had chosen other reading material that had been adapted into a movie or mini-series in order to introduce literary analysis concepts such as characterization, events advancing the plots, types of plot, foreshadowing, and tone. My students engaged in conversations about how the differences changed the meaning, or tone of events, or affected elements of characterization.

In addition to drawing from students' existing knowledge of the *Harry Potter* movies, I used audio books during the *Harry Potter* project to help support students' reading. I chose to use the audio books because my students do not have the decoding skills or reading stamina that would allow them to read the book independently. Students read along with the audio books, making accessible a book that would otherwise have been out of reach.

The audio books provided a model of fluent reading for students as they followed along in the book, which is an effective method used to develop fluency in struggling readers. I wanted my students to experience the story being read with all of the appropriate intonations, pauses, and use of tone. I wanted them to hear the rhythm and drama that can be created with words.

I think the greatest benefit of the tapes was that the unfamiliar voice that came from the stereo opened up a world of human drama that, although fantastical, explored the similar challenges we all face while trying to negotiate through the world. Many of my students also appreciated being able to listen to the story because I think that the tapes created a new listening experience for them. They had not heard a book on tape since early elementary school and I think many were surprised that the experience could be entertaining and enjoyable. Some of the students even asked to have the tracks loaded onto their iPods so they could listen to them at home.

The class typically began each lesson in the *Harry Potter* project with a summary of the previous listening/reading session, during which we would highlight any major events that affected the plot. I asked students to make predictions about what they thought would occur next in the story, and we charted them on the board so we could revisit them later. We listened to the audio book for about 15 minutes at a time, sometimes longer depending on the mood of the group.

Students were allowed to choose their own seating while listening. Two boys chose to sit next to the stereo. They enjoyed the experience of being about to control the volume and start and stop the tape at the appropriate times. They were responsible for starting the tape where we left off, as well as rewinding to the appropriate places when asked. Other students chose to lounge on the beanbags that were located near our classroom library. Some students chose to remain in their regular desks out of fear they would fall asleep on the beanbag!

As we listened to the audio book, students followed along in the book. I taught them to annotate the text using meta-cognitive markers.[6] Students were given either a specific marker to use while listening or more general guidelines for annotating the text. For example, some students were asked to use three markers in their text during the listening session. The class later shared the markers made while reading and discussed any major events that occurred in the story. We also revisited students' predictions; students were able to share the basis for their predictions and we highlighted the predictions that proved to be accurate.

The level of participation varied: some students diligently followed along and tracked the text while listening; others focused more on listening to catch discrepancies between the text and the film. All of the students listened carefully enough so they could contribute to the discussion that followed. The opinion-based discussion provided students with an opportunity to voice informed opinions—as opposed to just making factual statements, and to agree or disagree with statements from the peers using evidence from the text.

In addition to class discussions, the lesson typically closed with a writing task, either a response to a quote or a prompt for students to share their reactions to the most recent exploits of Harry or the character of their choice. When given a choice to write about a character, most students chose to write about Harry, with the exception of a few girls who wrote primarily about Hermione. These girls, on average, performed better academically and behaviorally than the other students and strongly identified with Hermione in the beginning of the book.

My students proved to be adept at making text-to-self connections through their reading of *Sorcerer's Stone*, contributing comments such as:

"Harry's life is messed up like our lives are messed up sometimes."

"Even though this story is made up, Harry has problems like kids like us."

"Sometimes being different can help you, but people still bother you for it."

"Sometimes being afraid can give you a reason to do good."

"My text-to-self connection is Harry is a bad-ass and I am a bad-ass too!"

My goals with each of the extension activities—the predictions, meta-cognitive markers, and writing prompts—were to give students opportunities to imagine what might happen in the story and to respond to the story elements as we encountered them.

I wanted the student take-away of the project to be the understanding that they are able to read a book, and have long and interesting conversations about what they've read. I wanted to share that experience with them since it did not appear they had ever had a similar experience before. I didn't feel like the journals would really provide complete evidence of any growth. While the students were able to talk about complex ideas, they still did not really have enough experience with writing to really be able to express themselves fully. The student learning markers for me were my observations about who spoke, the types of things that were said, and whether the ideas they shared were more developed than the responses they usually shared in class. For example, I had a female student in this class who was presumed to not be very smart, both by other students and many adults on campus. She, however, was one of the most vocal students in the class sharing her reactions and interpretations of the events in the book, and her personal connections to Harry. She immediately identified with his character over their similar feelings of being alienated from their foster families. This connection provided a deep hook for her into the book. It motivated her to work through her challenges to read so that she could read ahead at home. She was only reading at about a second-grade reading level, but she felt like she had found a text that was relevant to her life, and she wanted to read it so badly.

Allegra engaged with her students' needs for support in reading and used their familiarity with other media/technology to scaffold the reading assignment. More important, the reading activities were holistic, encouraging understanding, questioning, and critique of the story and its themes, as well as enjoyment of reading in general. The structure of her reading sessions mirrors Readers Workshop in that students sit where and how they like while reading. They were also deeply engaged with the text, including dialoguing about story events with each other and with Allegra. While her *Potter* project clearly encouraged deep engagement with the texts and connections to the knowledge and experiences that students already hold and value, it also supported Allegra's goal of making recreational reading an achievable, pleasant activity for her students.

Allegra's description of her classroom and student activities during the *Harry Potter* project also reflects what Cole and Griffin describe as "re-mediation,"[7] "a framework for the development of rich learning ecologies in which all students can expand their repertoire of practice through the conscious and strategic use of a range of theoretical and material tools."[8] This kind of advanced literacy is not generally expected of special education students; in her expectations for her students, Allegra was exceptional. Re-mediation is informed by sociocultural theories of learning, which emphasize the cultural and historical influences on a student's education, as well as the social nature of learning and literacy. Guiterrez and coauthors posit re-mediation as an alternative to traditional approaches to "remedial instruction," that is, strategies commonly used in schools to categorize and support students identified as different from the norm.[9]

The Battle for Hogwarts

A primary motivation for Allegra's selection of the *Harry Potter* series was her desire to provide her students with a reading experience that was enjoyable and meaningful. Her plan to read *Sorcerer's*

Stone together as a class and in its entirety was designed to introduce her students to the value of participation in a community of readers; independent reading does not foster the same level or types of engagement with a text that shared reading (especially shared reading of a popular book) can.

Parallel to this, the notion of creating a community around reading has become important to libraries aiming to better serve young patrons. In addition to changes to physical spaces in libraries, such as teen rooms or gaming centers, many school and public libraries have enhanced their collections of popular, alternative reading materials, including street lit,[10] graphic novels,[11] and manga,[12] in order to entice reluctant readers to leisure reading.

Allegra's use of fantasy literature is also different from the typical approach in urban public schools, and particularly those used with struggling readers of color. In her choices, she clearly expresses her disagreement with common assumptions about the types of materials that her students should engage with in order to improve their reading and their scores on standardized tests. A typical recommendation for reluctant readers in urban schools is to provide literature that realistically depicts life in the inner city. Hughes-Hassell and Rodge summarize the logic behind this recommendation:

> [Y]oung adult novels set in urban communities...offer confirmation and validation of the lives of urban youth, as well as legitimization of their inner-city cultures. The best of these books also counteract stereotypes of urban adolescents by creating characters that, in the details of their lives, challenge social expectations borne of stereotype. They do this by featuring adolescents who, for example, are successful in school and plan to attend college, understand and choose to avoid the dangers of drug use, and leave gang life behind.[13]

Based on the desire to provide "culturally relevant" texts, a growing collection of books about contemporary urban life for teens, for example, *Monster*,[14] *The House on Mango Street*,[15] and *The First Part Last*,[16] have become the "go to" choices for many teachers working with urban students of color.[17] As Ratner notes, the inclusion of these books is an important step in counteracting the ways in which "...today's inner-city students...are often misrepresented, underrepresented, or not represented at all in the literature typically offered in the high school classroom."[18]

Although realistic novels are often chosen as reading materials in multicultural classrooms, the place of realism in children's literature (and, indeed, children's media in general) is contested. While proponents of realistic literature highlight its strengths in "model[ing] the tools that children need to begin understanding their own relationship to reality and to literature,"[19] critics of realism in children's literature cite depictions of violence and mature themes such as drug use or sexuality as problematic for young readers. Realistic literature (and media) that engage with such topics is thought by critics to contribute to "hurried childhoods"[20] and perpetuate an image of a world under siege in which there are no happy families, no safe spaces for play, no childhood innocence.[21] Fantasy literature is presented as an alternative to gritty realism in children's stories. Allegra expresses similar concerns about her students becoming "overwhelmed" by themes that closely mirror their everyday experiences, not because she believes that as children they should be kept in the dark about such issues, but because many of her students, because of their learning disabilities, have diminished capability for critically assessing the messages in what they read. Carefully chosen fantasy, on the other hand, provides students who are learning to analyze literature with opportunities to observe, think about, and discuss difficult topics at arm's length.

In the book *Killing Monsters*, Gerard Jones, a longtime children's television producer and advocate, notes the strength of fantasy violence as a "crucial tool in accepting the limits of reality,"[22] which can contribute to helping children learn to cope with feelings and fears. Writing specifically about magic in children's literature, Alison Lurie points to links between fantasy and real-life needs and fears:

> Though we tend to take it for granted, the importance of magic in juvenile literature needs some explanation. Why, in a world that is so wonderful and various and new to them, should children want to read about additional, unreal wonders? The usual explanation is a psychological one: magic provides an escape from reality or expresses fears and wishes. In the classic folktale, according to this theory, fear of starvation becomes a witch or a wolf, cannibalism an ogre. Desire shapes itself as a pot that is always full of porridge, a stick that will

beat one's enemies on command, a mother who comes back to life as a benevolent animal or a bird. Magic in children's literature, too, can make psychological needs and fears concrete; children confront and defeat threatening adults in the form of giants, or they become supernaturally large and strong; and though they cannot yet drive a car, they travel to other planets.

Magic can do all this, but it can do more. In the literary folktale, it often becomes a metaphor for the imagination.[23]

Reading through this passage from Lurie's book on subversive children's literature, one can identify a number of these exact metaphors that are featured in the *Harry Potter* series. Indeed, several authors writing about the *Potter* series have noted its use of fairy tale conventions to touch upon real childhood fears and struggles. Notably, a *New York Times* article published shortly after the release of *Prisoner of Azkaban*, highlights the themes of parental abandonment and victimization, noting that Harry's physical weakness and broken glasses, as well as his unwelcoming accommodations in the Dursleys' home, reflect feelings of powerless and unease with which many children struggle to cope.[24] Allegra draws on similar powerful images to draw out her students' participation and grow their confidence as thoughtful readers:

It was assumed [by the administration] that teachers would want to read fiction with their students, and we were cautioned to limit the amounts of fiction our students were reading because students were scoring poorly on the test sections using informational text.

I think that the greatest challenge facing older students who do not read at grade level is that it is very difficult to make reading an enjoyable experience. The students are acculturated to understand that information to answer questions can be found in text, and that text can be used as a means to an end. For the students in my class, text was not seen as a source of entertainment; that seems to be a realm restricted to iPods, video games, and television—visually and aurally engaging media.

The emphasis on informational reading is directly connected to standardized testing requirements. The goal of the test is to read and answer questions. Therefore, during professional developments and staff meetings, a great deal of time was devoted to strategies for preparing students to take the CST [California Standards Test], which in terms of the English portion means reading to find the answer. School wide, students were coached to read the comprehension questions before reading the passage so they would know specifically what information required their attention. I don't feel like my students had a sense of reading for understanding or reading to get the gist until I made it a priority in my instruction.

In addition to the focus on informational reading, teachers at [my school] are urged to choose "culturally relevant" reading materials for our students. The book that was referenced the most as being "culturally relevant" for my students was Walter Dean Myer's *Monster*, which is about a 16-year-old Black boy being tried for felony murder. My objection to the book is entirely around the abstract messaging about its "relevance" and not with the text itself. I read the book as a youth and loved it. My concern with reading this text with my students was that I was teaching within a context where 16-year-olds were being incarcerated, sometimes for violent crimes. Almost all of my students had a close family member incarcerated, and a limited few had juvenile records already in the seventh grade. My trepidation was compounded by the response many students had to serving time; they feared and also revered their peers who had been to juvenile detention. The culture around incarceration overwhelmingly was not that it was a restrictive situation, but a rite of passage in a sense. For the boys at [my school], there was not a great fear around going to jail because it was something that occurred so often around them. My internal dialogue around reading this book in class centered around whether this text would play into these particular views about incarceration and substantiate their viewpoint that high rates of juvenile incarceration are normal or more specifically, something to be expected.

I continue to struggle with the idea of "culturally relevant" texts. I have not found a satisfying way to incorporate "culturally relevant" texts into my curriculum. I first tried to read stories with my students written by authors of color who wrote about issues that were closer to my students' lives: youth violence, drug use, disjointed families, life in economically depressed neighborhoods. The students were certainly able to make text-to-self-connections and talk about similar events in their lives. I did not, however, get the sense that these texts were cultivating their love for reading or helping them develop an understanding of the richness of text, which is what I wanted to convey to them.

Another issue that I have wrestled with is that many of my students are still developing the processing skills needed to look at situations that are similar to their own with an objective lens and to analyze all sides of the issues in novels that are typically deemed "culturally relevant" for poor students of color. Without the ability to pick apart these novels, I am concerned that students will feel overwhelmed by texts that depict negative or challenging situations that mirror aspects of their lives.

More importantly, I want my students to experience a text that is relevant to contemporary culture. *Harry Potter* has certainly carved out a space for itself in contemporary culture and I wanted my students to have firsthand experience with the text and create a meaning of the text for themselves. I feel that my students are not often directed towards fantasy-type novels. Reasons I assume for this are the students' developmental needs to establish themselves as no longer being kids and also the influence within education to expose our students to more serious, canonized literature as early as possible

I think that fantasy novels and books like the *Harry Potter* series are ideal to read with struggling readers because there is a very strong visual component to the stories. The story comes together in one's imagination, not in the words on the page. Youth culture today is engaged with strong visual images and the types of text that are going to hold students' attention are going to be the texts that engage that strong sense inside of them. Particularly for a struggling reader, the student needs to find something familiar in the process of reading to encourage them to continue with the laborious practice of decoding until it becomes automatic.

I do think that it is interesting that teachers do not look at fantasy novels as serious text, while so many of their students play fantasy and role-playing video games. If students are independently gravitating towards fantasy-type video games, directing them towards fantasy novels that share common themes could be an entry point for reluctant or disengaged readers.

Allegra's viewpoint on the importance of fantasy literature for struggling readers, including students in urban schools and special education students, is striking. Her choice to read fantasy fiction with her students served as a brave departure from typical school-assigned reading, which included very little fiction and instead emphasized skills for reading informational text such as those found on the required standardized tests. She noted that the students in her class did not regularly read books for pleasure: "the boys' independent reading material was mostly centered around video game and skating magazines. I saw groups of kids who did not interact with one another outside of class come together to go through the magazines and discuss game developments and cheating techniques." Her statement is consistent with the findings of a 2007 study of the leisure reading habits of urban adolescents, which found that unlike their suburban peers' reading preferences, urban teens' reading preferences were dominated by magazines.[25] Allegra decided to build on the interaction patterns that she observed introducing *Harry Potter* as a shared experience; students could talk about events in *Sorcerer's Stone* in the same way they shared ideas about gaming magazines.

Unfortunately, Allegra was unable to read *Sorcerer's Stone* with her students in its entirety. About halfway through the project, her school's administration mandated the use of a newly purchased scripted curriculum, effectively eliminating any opportunities that teachers had carved out for innovative lessons. Unsurprisingly, she was troubled by this change:

> As a teacher who has independently sought out professional development to be able to develop a balanced, holistic reading program for my students, it was very off-putting to be asked to suspend a reading unit that was focused entirely on engaging and entertaining students through text, to instead use a scripted program that has not shown to be effective with my population of students. There was nothing novel or specialized about the program that was purchased. It was just more worksheets, and "teacher proof" instructional guides that were intended for teachers that have no background knowledge in literacy development or accommodating for learning disabilities.
>
> My students have always been motivated by the topics that I show interest in and they trust my judgment in terms of what is useful information and what is not. I found it extremely difficult to hide my frustration with the scripted program, particularly since the curriculum covered skills I had already taught in much more inventive and contextualized ways. At first some students were motivated by the assignments because it was an opportunity for them to showcase some of the learning that took place the previous year (I follow my students from sixth grade to seventh grade), while others appreciated the

additional practice. However, as the weeks passed, it all just became passive activities that we engaged in for 54 minutes. The passivity is what upsets me the most. The last thing that I want as a teacher is to pass off passive interaction as learning. I wanted to get my students to a place where they expected more from school, and I feel like I had held them in that place in my classroom for almost two years, and then had to abandon it because my administrator mandated a ridiculous change and I was not at liberty to stand up against it.

It has taken me a few years to fully actualize my feelings about scripted curriculums. I have encountered some programs that have been very beneficial for middle school students with learning disabilities. However, as effective as sequenced, controlled, skill development activities are, students still need authentic reading experiences to use their newly developed skills. Also, students need to participate in authentic reading experiences so that they can begin to develop the stamina needed for sustained reading.

The tone of my class quickly changed when we stopped reading *Harry Potter*. Initially, my students were very unhappy that they had to suffer through another reading program and countless worksheets. They did seem to gain some comfort however in the familiar "read and answer the questions" format since it is something they were all conditioned well to do. Occasionally someone would make reference to the "time we listened to *Harry Potter*" and ask why we had to stop. When I reiterated that we stopped because this new program had been purchased for us, the students would just say "Oh, yeah" and shrug.

When we had to discontinue the project, about half of the students took the book home to continue reading. One student acquired a copy of the audio book on CD, and a few others tried to continue reading independently before becoming discouraged. Many did, however, re-watch the film during the project to search for details they had previously missed, or to scout for details in the novel that were missing from the film.

Had we had more time for this project, I wanted my students to write and record their own podcasts in response to developments in the plot. The girls enjoy giving each other endless advice about what they should have done in particular situations and I wanted to use the podcasts as a forum for them to give advice to the characters in the novel. I was going to make the project more open-ended for the boys, mostly because I have experienced that they are more

motivated by the element of choice. I can imagine that some may
have wanted to commentate the Quidditch games!

I was proud that I was able to facilitate something I find to be so
valuable for them. I was proud that they were willing to try something different, and be stretched in their thinking about what it
means to be different and whether it is possible that being different
can sometimes be a positive thing. I think my students began the
project with a very rigid idea about what it means to be in special
education: that it means that they were different from everyone else
and that something was wrong with them. I think that throughout
reading the novel several students were able to start to wrestle with
the understanding that they were in fact different, but that there
wasn't something inherently wrong with them.

I feel it really important to reassert to students in special education
that while there may be barriers that make them struggle with learning they are not stupid people. They need to be reminded constantly
that they are capable of learning anything, and there are particular
tools that best support their learning. It infuriates me how many students in special education really believe they are unintelligent. I am
equally infuriated by the number of adults who believe this about
these children and then rob them of their right to grow and learn in
school. However, my fury has helped to carry me through the work.
Working in special education can be very arduous and daunting at
times, but my frustration around all of these ideas about what a kid
in special education is like, or what a kid in special education can
accomplish, brings me back to why I do this work and why I think
it is important.

At my new school we follow a full inclusion model and I work
out of the Learning Center, out of which we provide special education and RTI [Response to Intervention] services. The model is both
push in and pull out. I have stocked the Learning Center library
with several *Harry Potter* books and I am planning to push reading
Harry Potter for independent reading or literature circles. Since my
new school serves mainly Latino students, I do wonder about how
the students would respond. I don't have any immediate plans to
read the book whole class, but rather as a tool to build relationships
with particular students.

Allegra's story calls attention to particular skills required of special
education teachers. As one would expect, she is an expert at specific

intervention techniques; however, it is the other skills that Allegra highlights—choosing fantasy literature, engaging everyday technologies to support student learning, critically assessing "culturally relevant" readings for the specific students in her classroom—that sets her philosophy for teaching special education apart from others.

The Hero in Special Education

In this final section of the chapter, we return to the *Potter* texts themselves to consider the ways in which the books address (and overlook) special education. Indeed, special education as we recognize it in U.S. schools is not part of Hogwarts' curriculum. Although characters are presented as having individual strengths and weaknesses, there appears to be no institutional system for obtaining extra help or alternate instruction. It is the student-run Dumbledore's Army that provides most students with extended coaching and customized instruction for the first time. While we as readers do not know much about most students in the school beyond their interactions with Harry, there are indicators that most students at Hogwarts are neither struggling academically nor dealing with emotional or behavioral challenges. For example, the race for house points is never won by a landslide, cohorts appear to move through the school intact (barring the occasional murder by Lord Voldemort), and Harry seems to be the only student regularly assigned to detention or prohibited from attending Hogsmeade trips.

Other *Potter* researchers have considered the possibility of Hogwarts students having learning disabilities. In particular, Mille Gore, a special education professor, has described Neville Longbottom as a "prototypical child with a learning disability, whether in the real world in which I exist, or in the fantasy world of *Harry Potter*."[26] Indeed, Neville's struggles to learn new spells or complete potions assignments look quite similar to students who are referred to special education for specific problems in their reading or mathematical abilities. In addition to Neville, one could consider Luna Lovegood's aloof behavior, nontraditional beliefs, and fixations similar to those of a high-functioning autistic student or a student with Aspberger's syndrome.

Often overlooked in discussions of special education, the Hogwarts student who best fits the profile of a special education student is Harry. At a very basic level, Harry has two of the very few physical disabilities that persist in the Wizarding world—poor eyesight and a cursed scar. Healing in the Wizarding world is extremely advanced, with cures existing for physical ailments from the common cold to hex-induced acne. Lasting bodily damage appears to result only from serious curses, such as the one that created Harry's famous lightning bolt scar, the one that charred Dumbledore's hand, or Bill Weasley's werewolf scars. Mad Eye Moody's physical disabilities, including his missing leg and eye, are the cumulative effect of years of serious curses. In a world where the school nurse can regrow bones, it is no surprise that we see no students who need wheelchairs or other health-related supports.

In the Muggle world, Harry might also be referred to special education for an emotional disturbance. The traumatic loss of his parents and subsequent abuses by his aunt and uncle as well as his constant state of mortal peril during his time as a student at Hogwarts certainly are ticks on the emotional disturbance checklist. Harry is the only student who has frequent outbursts in class (either due to temper or possession by Voldemort), and regularly gets into altercations with other students (most notably Malfoy) outside of the classroom.

Harry needs instruction that is different from the general magical curriculum. Like Neville, who needs extra help to master content, Harry too needs one-on-one support, extra time to practice, and encouragement from faculty to succeed in learning what he needs to survive. Unlike Neville, who receives this extra assistance from his peers only when he joins Dumbledore's Army, Harry receives extra help from a number of faculty members, including private lessons with Dumbledore and Snape and extra attention from his head of house and the fake Moody (for better or for worse). In terms of receiving instruction that is tailored to meet his special needs, Harry definitely is the "golden boy" at Hogwarts.

The *Potter* series' attention to issues of difference as well as Harry's special educational needs make it well suited for use in a special education classroom. Echoing Allegra's discussion of her choice to read *Sorcerer's Stone* with her students in order to give them some critical distance to reflect on their own lives, we believe that the *Potter* series offers important opportunities to talk specifically about the experience of being in special education—for teachers as well as for students. Certainly, using the series in special education presents particular challenges, including the length of the books, their complex vocabulary and intricate plots, and their departure from scripted curricula and expectations for RTI that define much of special education instruction, particularly in urban public schools. However, as Allegra has shown, given the right supports, students can benefit greatly from the experience of reading the books.

The next, and final, chapter of the book picks up on several of the themes that Allegra has highlighted here—choice (decision making), imagination, the importance of high expectations for educational experiences, and student participation. However, rather than looking at these issues through the reality of a classroom, as we have here and in Andrew and Sandra's chapters, we now turn to efforts outside of schools to promote learning and literacy in innovative ways.

Another Take on Teaching *Harry Potter*: On Being the Potions Professor

During the summer of 2007, I was in Washington, DC, for a professional development training on Engineering Academies with my principal, assistant principal and co-director. Little did they know the last *Harry Potter* book was going to be released at midnight on the last day. After the final seminar, I informed everyone I had to make a trip to the city. I quietly put on my *Harry Potter* glasses and boarded the Metro. One stop after I boarded, an older lady sat down across from me. She quietly leaned towards me and said "There are a lot of Muggles about tonight..."; then she got up and exited the train.

That night I went and bought the book, and spent all night reading. In the morning, my principal asked what I had done the night before and after I told her, she knew that I was truly a "potions professor" not just a teacher.

A few months later, the principal called me into her office to announce that she wanted our school to participate in the writing contest to attend a live reading for Los Angeles school district students given by J. K. Rowling. During an information session, one teacher informed me that two of the special day class students wanted to attend the reading. This would be the first time either student wrote an essay, and she wanted to make sure I knew they wrote at a lower level than other students their age. Both students made several drafts before entering their final essays, which in the end, I am proud to say, proved more meaningful and heartfelt than many of those written by the general education students.

On the day of the reading, every student selected, as well as all the adults, dressed in cloaks and hats, and stood out from the Muggles on their way to school. These two students in particular had not only the opportunity to hear an amazing author read a phenomenal passage, they were able to participate in an academic competition and be rewarded for what they had to say.

As a high-school chemistry teacher, my students are primarily graded on formulas and correct answers, not writing style. This was the first time I was able to really see what a positive impact the *Harry Potter* books have made, not just in terms of fun reading material but in truly motivating students.

Dana
Chemistry teacher and Potions Professor, public high school, Los Angeles, 6 years experience.

Chapter 7

Imagining More

*Imagination is not only the uniquely human capacity to envision that which is not, and therefore the fount of all invention and innovation. In its arguably most transformative and revelatory capacity, it is the power that enables us to empathise with humans whose experiences we have never shared...**We do not need magic to change the world, we carry all the power we need inside ourselves already: we have the power to imagine better.**[1]*

July 2007 has been called the "Summer of Potter,"[2] owing to the fact that the fifth movie and the final book were released within weeks of one another. For fans, these mass media events were punctuated by numerous other events within local communities and online, including conferences, concerts, podcasts, meet ups, and much more. It was during the Summer of Potter that we met at a unique conference designed for families to explore the world of *Harry Potter*. The conference, Enlightening 2007 (E7), was organized by a non-profit group called Bonding Over Books and was held on the campus of the University of Pennsylvania, right in the heart of West Philadelphia. About 150 families (350 people in total) from across the country attended. Unlike other Harry Potter conferences and events, which are usually designed by and for adults, E7 featured programming for kids aged 5 to 12 (divided into first through fifth years), and for teens aged 13 to 17. Much of the programming was also designed to encourage families to participate together.

Only the blistering Philadelphia heat indicated that we were not, in fact, at Hogwarts. For three days, Houston Hall was our castle, our school, and our playground. Its Great Hall featured floating candles and owl post, the classrooms were accessible by creaky staircases, the Room of Requirement provided supplies for an impossible number of concurrent activities. A short hop away lay the "Pennitch Pitch," where intense organized and pickup games of a sport similar to Quidditch were played. And, in the topmost tower of one of Penn's freshman dorms, teens enjoyed their own (stiflingly hot) common room.

Entire families arrived in costume, kids clutching the invitation letter that they had received in the mail some weeks prior. Despite the 100-plus degree heat, many young participants insisted on wearing their school robes all weekend. Wands were "at the ready." First through fifth years attended classes modeled after those taught at Hogwarts. For example, in astronomy, students drew their own constellations and described the meaning behind them. Divination class challenged students to solve a set of mysteries/logic puzzles using various clues modeled after psychic techniques. Kids read tea leaves, rearranging the letters on the leaves to spell out the answer to a clue. In potions class, students made concoctions (some edible!) that would have made Professor Snape's greasy hair curl. These recreations of the Hogwarts curricula were rounded out by activities drawn from the vibrant world of *Harry Potter* fan culture ("fandom"), including a session focused on developing the language of media critique through critical reviews/discussion of the fifth film, and a fan fiction writing (and illustration) workshop.

E7 was the first *Harry Potter* event of its kind; it was an incredible labor of love for its creators and staff. By the end of the weekend, friendships were forged, not only between kids attending the conference but also within families, as parents and children were able to connect over a shared interest. (It would, of course, be an exaggeration to claim that all families had this experience; there were certainly families who found themselves in competing houses, as well as parents accused of "dark magic.") With very few exceptions, everyone gave themselves over to the magic of the weekend, making themselves open to participate, explore, and play with the story in very special ways. Film theorists would say that we suspended our disbelief—agreed to go along with the version of reality that we were seeing at the time—others would call it role playing; whatever it was, for that weekend, we were wizards.

*   *   *

It is fairly easy to look at an event such as E7 and identify it as an opportunity for learning; it is also fairly easy to look at the organizers and identify them as literacy advocates. Their desire to create a space and opportunity for families to "bond over books" (as the name of the organization states) was a unique idea, particularly at a time when children's literacy and uses of popular culture, media, and technology are increasingly divisive within many American families.[3] E7's focus on the social and emotional connections that can be forged through shared experiences of literature, its treatment of reading as an essential part of everyday family life, and its emphasis on the pleasures of sharing a great story with significant others are quite different from the phonics drills and comprehension questions that make up much of the reading practice in schools. However, the approach to literacy seen at E7 resembles more closely the relationships the *Teaching Harry Potter* teachers crafted with their students while reading *Harry Potter* in their classrooms.

In addition to its focus on family literacy, E7 was special because of its dedication to media literacy—it picked up on the advice issued in the books: to avoid underestimating children's stories, to approach every story critically, to search for truth, to create equal opportunities for expression, and to approach books and reading less instrumentally (searching for the answer to a multiple-choice question) to instead create a space one can inhabit, and in which one can make friends, learn, and write one's own stories.

E7 was also special because of its experiential and shared educational experiences. In recreating Hogwarts-style classes, organizers created rich, teachable moments driven by the kids' interests as participants engaged in creating and learning about something they connected with, loved, and found valuable. Progressive educator John Dewey would have thoroughly enjoyed E7. Were he alive today, he would certainly look to such an experience as evidence that joy in learning is still possible. Writing some 50 years prior, he called for very similar pedagogical approaches:

> Now see to it that day by day the conditions are such that *their* [students'] *own activities* move inevitably in this direction, toward such culmination of themselves. Let the child's nature fulfill its own destiny, revealed to you in whatever of science and art and industry the world now holds as its own.[4]

E7 stands in stark contrast to traditional school experiences, and moves in a completely different direction from current trends in educational policy, as we have discussed throughout this book. Returning again to J. K. Rowling's 2008 commencement speech at Harvard University, we see direct connections between experiences such as E7 and her call to "imagine better," for the world. Although E7 was a small-scale event, experienced by only a few hundred students, it was a powerful learning experience that should be viewed as a model for future immersive educational experiences. It provides a start toward imagining better for the world, not an end point.

We have titled this chapter "Imagining More" as a way to connect to Rowling's charge for change in the world as well as to emphasize the great need to consider issues of scale and equity when we consider innovative educational experiences and literacy programs. "Imagining More" speaks to the unfinished and unequal nature of immersive educational experiences like E7; they are wonderful and valuable experiences for students who can access them. The next step is figuring out how to open opportunities for participation more widely. How do we translate principles from immersive experiences like E7, where reading the books is only the first step to learning and engagement, to schools like those in which Sandra, Andrew, and Allegra teach? Is this even possible or advisable? And, what other models should we look to when imagining more for our schools and students?

Encouraging Participation in Schools

"Oh, the bus don't go to Hogwarts.
You gots to take the train.
No, the bus don't go to Hogwarts.
You gots to take the train.
And we'll take the train from Platform $9^{3/4}$.
And we'll take the train from Platform $9^{3/4}$!
'Cause the bus don't go to Hogwarts;
You gots to take the train!"[5]

Harry Potter fans have mainly operated separately from schools for all the reasons that we have laid out in the earlier chapters of this book—school structures that limit time, access to media, curriculum, as well as cultural/representational issues (real or assumed), interests, objections to the content of the books, cultural capital—and, undoubtedly, myriad other reasons not mentioned here. Many of the features and practices of fandom—its intergenerational social structure, its roots in mass media and consumer culture, its innovative uses of technology, and its subversion of normative ideology, for example—seem, on the surface, wholly incompatible with the current context of schooling.

Rather than giving in to the frustration of a seemingly insurmountable mismatch between the participatory culture of fandom and that of public schooling, we wish to raise a number of questions about why such a mismatch exists, what our goals should be in terms of opening up participation to a wider group of students, and what the specific roles of teachers and schools might be in a re-imagined learning environment. As readers will see, we have far more questions than answers at this point, including the following: How might schools and organizations such as those that make up the core of the *Harry Potter* fandom adjust in order to find opportunities for overlap? Can participatory experiences such as E7 be opened to students who do not necessarily see themselves as "readers" or "fans?" And, if they can, how do we best manage the translation and scaling of such experiences? What can be done to bring greater access to high-poverty, immigrant, and/or marginalized students? For those who do gain access, how can that experience be enhanced and how can students be encouraged to continue participating on their own?

If, as we argue earlier in this book, schools are to remain an important venue for access to information, culture, and opportunities for learning and civic participation, then it is essential to push past roadblocks such as standardized curricula and punitive testing to encourage innovation and connection to learning in the world outside of school. As Henry Giroux writes:

> When educational reform neglects matters of politics, critical thinking, creativity and the power of the imagination, it loses its hold on preparing young people for a democratic future and condemns them to a world where the only values that matter are individual acquisition, unchecked materialism, economic growth and a winner-take-all mentality.[6]

The picture of neglect that Giroux paints here is, unfortunately, more common than not in U.S. public schools at present, particularly where critical thinking is concerned.

It seems that what *Harry Potter* fans understand that "school," as an American institution, does not (at least not very well) is that literacy is not (and never really has been) *just* about books or words on a page. *Potter* fans understand that literacy is social; that much of the enjoyment of reading and many of the opportunities for deep understanding of what one reads comes from sharing the experience of reading with others. Literacy cannot be understood simply as something that happens in the head of an individual, but should also attend to the shared experiences of a community. This is how books (and other media) come alive. Indeed, the *Harry Potter* series stands as an excellent resource for illustrating the concept of literacy as the interaction of readers and texts; texts—notably, *The Monster Book of Monsters*, *Tom Riddle's Diary*, and the *Marauder's Map*—literally come alive in Harry's world. Sharing information from different types of books, from textbooks such as *Hogwarts, a History* to children's books such as *The Tales of Beedle the Bard*, becomes central to solving mysteries and, ultimately, to saving the world from evil.

Clearly, Rowling understands and believes in literacy as a shared and social practice.

Particularly in the twenty-first century, where media surrounds us, it is also essential for schools to have a better understanding of how literacy operates *between* and *across* media. As we discussed in Chapter 5, the participation gap between students (and teachers) with access to new media, and those genres of participation conducive to learning, and those without access to these tools and opportunities remains a major threat to educational and social equity. The importance of learning to read multiple types of media adds another layer of challenge to the work of schools.

As we saw in the teachers' chapters, each teacher acted as a gatekeeper for her or his students, using their keys to open wide the gates to literacy. For various reasons, students were not accessing books (*Harry Potter* books or otherwise) on their own, so the teachers stepped in to guide the experience and encourage students to persevere in reading these difficult texts. In the cases that Sandra, Andrew, and Allegra presented, their approaches proved highly successful—their students were able to read (at least part of) a book that was meaningful, entertaining, and challenging. They were also able to demonstrate their learning as they shared the experience with their classmates in critical discussions.

Teachers *can* and *should* take on the role of gatekeeper for their students, but only to open widely and permanently the gates in place. Teachers cannot be the sole suppliers of literacy. Imagine if every book you ever read were chosen for you by someone else. No matter how smart or well intentioned that person, you would certainly miss out on resources and experiences that might prove to be valuable. Students must get to the point where they have enough confidence in their reading abilities and have had enough opportunities to develop their own interests to seek out books, magazines, websites, and other media on their own, with neither the threat of comprehension questions nor the constant encouragement of a teacher to keep them turning the pages. Students need to discover their passions and need to know how to investigate them. They need to become literate, self-assured, lifelong learners. This is not to say that support is unimportant, that learners need to be totally independent and self-directed, or that there are not many obstacles to literacy. However, most would agree that one of the primary goals of schooling is to prepare students to be informed, engaged, caring, thoughtful, and satisfied adults, as opposed to the self-interested and single-minded consumers that Giroux describes, and that this goal cannot be reached unless students are both allowed and challenged to be equal partners in their literacy and learning.

Next, we discuss the ways in which *Harry Potter* readers have responded to the rally cry for critical media literacy issued in the books and the ways in which their actions can be understood as "imagining more." Like the work Sandra, Allegra, and Andrew engaged in with their students, readers look to the books for a literary experience that explains the world, basks in the pleasures of reading, and incites passion and imagination. The quote that begins this section is from a song called "Platform 9 and ¾," written and performed by a band called Harry and the Potters, the pioneers of a musical genre called Wizard Rock (discussed later in the chapter). The genre is made up of an ever-growing number of bands that write and perform songs (in various styles) about *Harry Potter*. We selected the quote for a number of reasons. For one, it speaks to the experiential and imaginative aspects of what readers do in reading these books. You cannot get to Hogwarts just any old way—you have to be willing to imagine what it is like to take the Hogwarts Express from a secret platform at King's Cross Station over the hills to an unplottable magical space. You have to give yourself over to the fantasy of the books. The line "We'll take the train from Platform 9 and $^{3/4}$", then, is an affirmation that readers will buy into the story. They will take the experience and run with it. On another note, looking at the song and the *Harry Potter* readership through an equity lens, we are mindful of another interpretation. The way to get to Hogwarts lies through a privileged means of transport (a magical high-speed train!); the bus, public transport ostensibly accessible to everyone, will not get you there. We cannot accept this—our goal must be to get the bus to stop at Platform 9 and $^{3/4}$—which, if you think about it, is what the *Teaching Harry Potter* teachers accomplished.

Next, we will examine a few examples of *Potter* literacy taking place outside of schools. We argue that most *Harry Potter* fans could be called literacy advocates because of their commitments to promoting reading, modeling critical literacy, and exemplifying the social aspects of literacy. We feature a few special cases, highlighting the ways in which *Harry Potter* readers and fans have navigated the sticky terrain of learning with popular culture. In particular, we consider two related and important movements within fandom: Wizard Rock and the Harry Potter Alliance (HPA). Both represent creative, distributed approaches to advocacy and powerful examples of "imagining better." The HPA is particularly important to our discussion as it provides a mechanism for channeling some of the momentum of fandom-based participation back to schools. To conclude, we return to the *Teaching Harry Potter* teachers to consider their efforts in the context of these larger, participation-based activities. How can similar meaningful and engaging experiences be made accessible to all readers?

We have positioned these stories here, at the close of our book, in order to gesture at what we see as one possible future for teaching. While schools are increasingly narrowed, alternative spaces encourage creativity and make it possible for learners to interact with ideas that they find interesting—through imagination, virtual tools, or, as in the case of E7, in exchange and sharing with others. Throughout this book, we carefully consider the implications of incorporating popular culture into diverse, urban public school classrooms. We look to the teachers' expertise on how to make a story that seems, at first blush, far removed from the students' (or teachers') situations feel meaningful and relatable. In looking outside of schools for additional guidance, though, we do not abandon them; we instead recognize that for traditional public schools, the road to utilizing these participatory modes of learning and participation is quite long. Schools cannot immediately *apparate* (move from one place to another instantly) away from their locked-down, standardized modes of operation—at least not on their own. Therefore, we consider this chapter an opportunity for *side-along apparition*—an opportunity to explore alternate possibilities together.

Fight Evil. Read Books: Wizard Rock and the Promotion of Literacy

In our opinion, *Harry Potter* fans provide quintessential models of the kinds of active reading that should be taught and encouraged in schools. The release of the *Potter* books, films, video games, and licensed merchandise coincided with the maturation of the Internet and the development of the social Web, both important new spaces for development, distribution, and participation with popular culture. The very timing of the *Potter* series supported the growth of a large, vibrant, and diverse online fandom.[7] Fan participation, which ranges from online discussions and reading groups to Do-It-Yourself (DIY) media production, fits nicely with an alternative (but complementary) definition of popular culture. As media theorist John Fiske describes, popular culture is not necessarily the products people buy, but the way they use them in their everyday lives:

> The creativity of popular culture lies not in the production of commodities so much as in the productive use of industrial commodities. The art of the people is the art of "making do." The culture of everyday life lies in the creative, discriminating use of the resources that capitalism provides.[8]

Fiske arrived at this understanding of popular culture as "making do" through his research on punk bands. Harry and the Potters, the band quoted at the beginning of this chapter, cites punk music as one of its musical and ideological influences, and clearly exemplifies the DIY ethic captured in the idea of "making do." As the pioneers of Wizard Rock, a diverse genre of music linked not by style but by content,[9] Harry and the Potters has been instrumental in promoting a unique, creative, and popular form of advocacy among *Harry Potter* fans. The band consists of two brothers, Paul and Joe DeGeorge, who write and perform songs as Harry Potter—one as Harry in year four and one as Harry in year seven. This anachronism allows them to play with point of view in their songs, which range from simple tunes about elements of the books, such as the one quoted at the beginning of this chapter, to more politically charged songs such as "Voldemort Can't Stop the Rock," which begins with the announcement that the song is about "sticking it to the man." Following this statement, partially for performative reasons and partially (we think) in recognition of the varied ages of their fans, DeGeorge asks the audience if they know who "the man" is. In the case of Harry Potter, "the man" is Voldemort, but, as they remind their audiences, "the man" is anyone who champions evil and keeps love out of the world.

Wizard Rockers and their fans can be understood as a new breed of literacy advocates. Rather than locating their argument for reading the books in a class-based, exposure to "classics" argument, they focus on the social and fun aspects of being a part of a literary community. Wizard Rock concerts are almost always free unless they are charity fundraisers or need to cover venue rental costs. Initially, libraries were the primary venues for concerts, as they reinforced the commitment to literacy and public access.

In addition, some Wizard Rock bands, Harry and the Potters again being the first among these, use their music to communicate political messages—fight evil, read books, be proud of who you are, be brave. Andrew Slack, the head of the Harry Potter Alliance (another unique advocacy group we will discuss further in a moment), described the basic philosophy of the Wizard Rock movement as encouraging wide and diverse participation. He noted a general agreement that there is no such thing as "bad" Wizard Rock—the important part is creating a space and mode of expression and connection with other fans, not the technical proficiency of the music itself. From its early days, Harry and the Potters has encouraged wide participation; for example, Paul DeGeorge, the older of the two Harrys, signed CDs with the charge "start your own band," a simple statement encouraging any fan—regardless of age or musical experience—to join in the movement. Clearly, fans took his (and others') encouragement to heart, as there are now several hundred Wizard Rock bands in existence.[10]

Wizard Rock has been incredibly successful in opening a different kind of participation in *Harry Potter* fandom. Using popular music has drawn in teenaged fans who participate in ways (and numbers) never before seen. Furthermore, because one can listen to and enjoy

Wizard Rock without having to have read the books, it opens opportunities for participation to younger children and, potentially, non-readers. Wizard Rock provides an entry point to the intensive and enjoyable intellectual and social experiences characteristic of participation in fan culture for a much wider group of people, including welcoming boys and teens into a space that has long been dominated by white, middle-class, adult women.[11]

The increased participation of teens has changed the dynamic of fandom (for better or for worse, depending on who you ask), but importantly, it has made it clear that *Harry Potter* does not "belong" to any one group of people. If we consider the challenges that the *Teaching Harry Potter* teachers faced in convincing and reassuring their students that the books were not just for "white people," that they could (and should) be read in Spanish, or that there are connections between the Wizarding world and the projects of Los Angeles, the work Wizard Rock has done in opening participation becomes that much more significant.

The song "Welcome to the House of Awesome," written and performed by a band called The Whomping Willows, is a powerful affirmation of Wizard Rock's commitment to opening participation in reading and fandom. Like Harry and the Potters, The Whomping Willows' music is an experiment in role play, as all of the songs are written from the point of view of the large, aggressive, magical tree on Hogwarts's grounds, affectionately called "Whompy" by the band and its fans. "Welcome to the House of Awesome" describes Whompy's reaction to his exclusion from the Hogwarts' student body. As the following excerpt of the lyrics shows, Whompy takes matters into his own hands and fights back:

> The students at Hogwarts are sorted into Houses according to
> Whatever that shifty Sorting Hat says they ought to do.
> I asked Dumbledore if I could be sorted.
> He said, "Sorry, Whompy, but I could get reported
> to the Ministry of Magic for incorrect procedure–
> You're not a wizard, you're a tree."
>
> So I'm starting a new House and it's called Awesome!
> I'm starting a new House and it's called Awesome!
> I'm starting a new House and it's called Awesome![12]

This song captures both the inclusive and the subversive spirit of the movement. Like many other Wizard Rock songs, the antiprejudice message is clear and simple enough for young fans to grasp. The song's commentary on the failure of the powers-that-be to address needs for diversity and inclusion is also evident, along with a model for action and advocacy. If you are marginalized by the rules in place, change the rules; start your own house and let everyone join.

*   *   *

Next, we turn to another example of advocacy emerging from the *Potter* fandom—the Harry Potter Alliance (HPA). The HPA has figured out the alchemy of participatory culture and traditional organizations such as schools. Its approach echoes one of the central themes throughout this book—the importance of localized, contextualized decision making. By encouraging and supporting chapters to participate in ways that make sense for them, to choose the service projects that best reflect the community in which a particular chapter is based, the HPA serves as a new model organization and an incredibly positive example for school-based literacy advocacy efforts.

What Would Dumbledore Do? The Harry Potter Alliance and Schools

Harry worries about who he is, but realizes that what he does matters most. And, I believe, so do the children reading the books.[13]

The HPA was formed in 2005 with help of Harry and the Potters. Like Wizard Rock, the HPA embraced a DIY ethic in its efforts as an advocacy organization. The idea behind the HPA was to create a version of Dumbledore's Army for the real world—a group of committed individuals who could work together to fight injustices and raise awareness of the evils in our world. In the five years of the organization's existence, it has launched a number of initiatives, including book drives for schools and libraries destroyed in hurricane Katrina and on-the-ground and online efforts to register new voters for the 2008 presidential election. Recently, the HPA (in conjunction with several other fandom-based organizations) raised more than $123,000 for supplies sent to Haiti following the devastating earthquake there in the spring of 2010.[14]

The HPA has a unique understanding of literacy that differs greatly from what is commonly taught in schools. It focuses on media literacy—specifically, New Media Literacies related to communication and collaboration using new media and transmedia navigation—and aims to use members' passions and familiarity with such literacy skills to incite action in the local and larger community. Essentially, the HPA seeks to activate smart, passionate people who want to change the world but need some structure to begin. As HPA Executive Director Andrew Slack told us in an interview, "People generally are new media and book literate, but not familiar with the concept of being an activist. Anyone can be an activist."

In terms of connections to schooling, the HPA is a useful example of employing popular culture that students already like and find interesting to motivate learning about other subjects and forge connections between information, experiences, and beliefs. The organization benefits from the wide readership of the *Potter* series and its in-text commitments to educational and social equity, fighting prejudice, developing confidence in one's abilities, and championing the power of love over evil. Motivation to participate in the HPA comes from people's existing interest in *Harry Potter*, the transition from thinking about the evils in the Wizarding world to those in our own world, therefore building on prior understanding and ideas derived from the reading experience. The HPA is one outlet that interested readers can use to channel their interest in *Harry Potter* into action: making or doing activities that complement their active consumption of the books. Whereas some fans write fan fiction or create podcasts to continue the story or debates beyond the books, HPA members extend the story through activism.

In our conversation with Andrew Slack, we discussed the challenges of finding and using students' passions in diverse classrooms, especially when the students do not hold the literacy skills characteristic of HPA members. It is unlikely that a teacher will ever have a classroom of students who are all passionate about the same topics or a classroom of students who all have the literacy skills and tools necessary to pursue them. He used the metaphor of alchemy to explain what he sees as the responsibility of educators to help students discover their interests and facilitate their ability to pursue them. Like an alchemist who finds gold in common minerals, teachers who "see the gold" in their students can help them figure out how to bring it forward.

A more concrete connection between the activities of the HPA and schools comes in the form of chapters. HPA chapters are local groups, each with their own leadership, that plan events within their own communities and participate as a group in the larger initiatives identified by the HPA board and staff. According to Karen Bernstein, an advisory board member and former Chapter Chair, there are four main configurations of chapters: community chapters made up of both adults and youth participants; community chapters run by high-school students who (for various reasons) chose to organize the chapter outside of the school; school-based chapters in high schools and middle schools; and collegiate chapters. While the HPA is not a school-based organization, students make up a substantial percentage of its membership.

As Karen described in our interview, the idea of having local HPA chapters originated with the membership itself. Participants desired a way to connect to other local members in order to work on projects in their own communities as well as organization-wide initiatives. High schools' requirements for student organizations, for example, having a leadership structure and a faculty advisor/mentor, were influential in shaping the structure of the chapters. In addition, Karen notes that she and her colleagues researched other organizations that blend on- and offline participation as well as local, national, and international participation, for example, the Peace Alliance and National Novel Writing Month. Echoing what Andrew Slack told us about motivating and guiding participation, Karen told us that "students often have the passion, but not the leadership experience." Therefore, the HPA staff focuses on helping members channel their passion into productive activities. Again, since members come to the chapter already caring about *Harry Potter*, extension to the issues highlighted by the HPA presents a natural and easy transition.

The chapter structure of the HPA highlights the value of agency in creating and maintaining a functional space for learning and participation. Chapters are supported step-by-step in their configuration and operation. Far from being prescriptive, however, HPA staff and resources emphasize that chapters should choose modes of participation that work best for their particular group. For example, chapters are required to check in regularly with the national office, but may do that in one of several ways, including e-mail or through regularly scheduled online meetings. Chapters are also encouraged to adapt their group organization and leadership as needed. For example, Karen recounted the story of a high-school chapter that was criticized by parents because of HPA's commitment to raising awareness of issues related to the gay, lesbian, bisexual, transgender, and queer (GLBTQ) communities and championing equal rights, including the legalization of gay marriage. Although the high-school chapter had chosen not to participate in projects related to this initiative itself, vocal critics demanded that the group be disbanded. With the help of HPA staff, the chapter quickly found a public library that was willing to sponsor the group and moved the chapter out of the purview of the school.

This example illustrates the kind of freedom that comes with allowing choice. Encouraging and supporting active decision making allows for the rich trial-and-error learning that learning scientists have emphasized for years. Failure is an option in the HPA—giving up and not learning from the experience, however, is not. As Karen noted in our interview, "I have no problem with a chapter having an event that fails as long as they feel they can come to us to talk about it afterward." These discussions provide an opportunity to assess what went wrong and make plans to address these issues in the future. In the above example, housing the chapter in that particular high school was not the right option. The organizers tried it and were not successful; however, rather than abandoning the idea of the chapter, their solid communication with HPA staff allowed them to adjust the plan and continue operating without missing a beat.

In addition to encouraging choice, Karen noted the teaching methods used by HPA staff in interacting with the chapter organizers (and members more generally). The methods that the HPA uses are different from what is typical in schools; as Karen told us, the focus is on providing useful resources and guiding conversations with chapter leaders (and teaching chapter leaders to guide conversations with their members) in order to make sure that chapters are directing their focus productively. In this way, the organization teaches not just about issues such as gay marriage, genocide, and corporate responsibility, but also teaches leadership and cultivates activists.

The HPA is an exceptional organization that has been recognized in the media and by J. K. Rowling herself. Celebrating its five-year anniversary in the fall of 2010, the group has already pulled off events and initiatives that much older organizations have not. Its unique approaches to organizing, commitment to media literacy, emphasis on both local and personal decision making, and a mentoring approach to teaching are characteristics schools could definitely draw from. The HPA is a model of twenty-first-century learning, and while it is not the only model, it stands as an especially strong one.

Imagining More

[The Mirror of Erised] shows us nothing more or less than the deepest, most desperate desire of our hearts. You [Harry], who have never known your family, see them standing around you... However, this mirror will give us neither knowledge or truth. Men have wasted away before it, entranced by what they have seen, or been driven mad, not knowing if what it shows is real or even possible.[15]

Harry's encounter with The Mirror of Erised (desire), while a cautionary moment within *Sorcerer's Stone*, also gives us a personal (and heartbreaking) look at Harry's deepest wish, to know his family. Although Dumbledore warns Harry not to lose himself in the fantasy portrayed in the mirror, we take the opportunity to use the mirror for our own purposes—cautiously, of course. Given all that has been discussed here, what would we—as educators and citizens concerned with the future of public education and the teaching profession—see were we to take a glimpse into the Mirror of Erised? With hopeful eyes, we take four glances.

Expert Teachers Engaged as Leaders and Trusted Professionals

Our first glimpse into the mirror would show us teachers acting on their own agency and freely utilizing their expertise in school and classroom decision making. In Chapter 1, we sketched out our vision of a "highly qualified" teacher based on the commonalities shared by the *Teaching Harry Potter* teachers. We would expect to see that these shared strengths—expert knowledge of the field, caring, resiliency, innovation, and a critical, culturally relevant approach— were not only supported but also given the space to grow and be shared with other teachers.

In *The Flat World and Education,* Linda Darling-Hammond details her recommendations for "Strong Professional Practice"[16] including "improving teacher recruitment and retention," "reinventing teacher preparation and development" in a manner that makes teacher education performance-based, and encouraging and rewarding "teacher and school leader knowledge and skill" through new career ladder models[17] that would create pathways that "should recognize skill and accomplishments, enable professionals to take on roles that allow them to share their knowledge, and promote increased skill development and expertise across the profession."[18]

In reading through their narratives (and, for our part, knowing them well), it is not difficult to imagine Sandra, Andrew, and Allegra engaging these opportunities to great effect. In our mirror, these teachers would be encouraged to grow and share their expertise with their students, colleagues, and administrators. Rather than being constrained in their teaching practices, they would find themselves positioned as mentors and creative teacher leaders within their schools. For example, Sandra would be recognized for her skill set and expertise and tapped to help frame the curricular goals for the students. She would serve as a teacher leader and mentor to new teachers at her school and be provided regular release time to observe and conference with those she was mentoring. In these roles, she would be enlisted in a proactive rather than a constantly reactive position. She would also be encouraged to innovate, to imagine and explore the possibilities for building on the learning community through technology and media projects. Most of all, she and her students could choose another book to read together without having to worry that they would not be allowed to finish it.

The *Teaching Harry Potter* teachers push boundaries and accomplish a great deal, but not without struggling to navigate around antiquated educational systems that limit, rather than grow, their capacity to effect meaningful change. We can only imagine what Sandra, Andrew, and Allegra—and others like them—could accomplish were they to work in an educational system that recognizes their expertise and trusts them to use it well. We hope that for now, parents, administrators, and policymakers will support such teachers and advocate for them whenever and wherever possible.

Universal Access to Technology and New Media as Learning Tools

In taking a second look into the mirror, we would see schools where media and technology are embedded, organic aspects of school life. As students' lives become ever more filled with media and technology, and as their everyday practices become ever more linked to the affordances of consumer electronics and digital media, schools must work harder to maintain relevance and provide students with the opportunities for learning and literacy that they need to succeed in the twenty-first century. Rather than seeing schools continue to "Polyjuice" educational media and technology—using it in insignificant and spurious ways—we would expect to see digital media used in a student-driven, creative, and integrated manner across the curriculum, throughout the school day, and in connection with other spaces in students' learning ecologies.

Andrew's broad use of media and popular culture in his classroom provides evidence of how these can be effectively integrated, even into college prep courses. In our mirror, the firewall he contends with daily is down and his students have ready access to the information and resources necessary to engage in critical research and discourse around popular texts, online media, and the canonical works they are assigned. Given all that Andrew's students accomplish with the firewall in place, our mirror shows an endless array of extraordinary learning moments possible with it removed.

Emphasis on Experiential, Student-Driven Learning

Our third look would show teachers and students engaging in experiential learning that derives from the students' interests, including popular culture, and extends beyond classroom and school walls. Like E7, these experiences could be immersive, enabling students to live out their ideas using internalized knowledge reframed to reflect their own vision of what they are learning. Here we turn again to John Dewey, who stated that

> ...if an experience arouses curiosity, strengthens initiative, and sets up desires and purposes that are sufficiently intense to carry a person over dead places in the future, continuity works in a very different way.
> Every experience is a moving force.[19]

These experiences would also include opportunities to work in the students' communities, using critical learning and media literacy to discern and research community needs and to engage in meaningful service projects. As the HPA demonstrates, these forms of learning fuel Dewey's "moving force." They are empowering in that students have control of the form and content of their educational process, enabling them to make choices about *what* and *how* they learn and contribute to their schools and communities.

The leadership, communication, and research skills practiced when engaging in these activities are invaluable tools for building confidence. This is evident in the accomplishments and growth of the HPA. Duncan-Andrade and Morrell describe a similar experience engaging in critical praxis with their students, "...when the curriculum begins with a problem or issue that is identified in collaboration with youth, there is no doubt as to its relevance or its authenticity."[20] Engaging students in the design, form, goals and process of education only serves to help them become more successful, confident learners and, as in the case of the HPA, leaders as well.

Authentic Tasks as the Central Form of Student—and Teacher—Assessment

Looking into the mirror a fourth time, we would find that as a result of teacher empowerment, fluid media and technology access, and a focus on experiential education, the heavy reliance on standardized testing and—in high-poverty urban settings—scripted curriculums would have been deemed inappropriate and unnecessary. The detrimental effects of such policies are clearly evidenced in Sandra's account, where she has been forced to narrow her teaching delivery to rote activities that "drill down" on her students' testing abilities. In doing so, she works against her own teacher intuition and wealth of experience. The same holds true for Allegra, whose professional expertise was undermined when she was forced to discontinue a unit that had obviously engaged her class, in favor of a scripted curriculum. The authentic projects planned for her students, who would have clearly benefited greatly from the ownership that such choices would bring them, were abruptly discontinued.

Instead, in our mirror, forms of authentic learning matching the goals and needs of the students while simultaneously challenging them to move far beyond basic levels of comprehension would be firmly in place. While a set of reasonable standards might remain, they would serve as base guidelines, as a set of "starter ideas" with which to anchor the curriculum rather than serve as the ultimate goal of schooling.

In the mirror, then, we might see students and teachers engaging in community service projects based in their own research, writing blogs to comment on a particular book that they are reading, preparing a performance of a student-written play, or presenting a portfolio of their academic growth in a particular subject over the course of the year. The possibilities for what could be produced are as numerous as the students themselves. We would see, for example, the podcasts that Allegra had planned as a summative assessment being produced and recorded by her students. We would see the class actively engaged and self-directed as they moved through the process. Eventually, they would share their efforts, thus presenting their ideas and opinions—in podcast form—to their peers and others. The students would grow in confidence and ability having completed the task—and we would see Allegra's guidance and design of the project recognized by her administrators as highly valuable.

* * *

The amazing things that we would see each time we looked in the mirror would certainly be difficult to turn away from, but in the end, we would need to heed Dumbledore's warning. We could sit and waste away simply allowing the mirror to speak to us. Eventually, though, we need to leave the room, allow the mirror to be hidden away, and begin to act on our beliefs and desires. It is time to not only imagine more but also to use one's voice in the effort to support teachers and students who need it most.

J. K. Rowling has talked repeatedly about the power of love serving as the central theme of the *Potter* books. In an essay commenting on *Harry Potter and the Half-Blood Prince*, critic Lev Grossman wrote:

> Love is much more important to Rowling than magic. The real mystery, for her, is the human heart. She has always been more interested in the hand that wields the wand, the way the enchantment illuminates the wizard who casts it.[21]

Indeed, Lily Potter's love protects her son Harry as he grows to adulthood, the love of his mentors brings him strength and guidance, and the love of his friends saves his life numerous times, ultimately giving him the strength to persevere against death. On the other hand, love is the one thing that Voldemort cannot understand and therefore underestimates. His refusal to acknowledge its power and potential ultimately leads to his downfall. In many ways, our educational system suffers from the same shortsightedness.

Nel Noddings, who writes extensively on caring in education, describes the current "insistence on more and more testing" as "largely a product of separation and lack of trust" between parents and teachers and teachers and their students who cannot form caring relationships under such pressures to perform. She states:

> Then fear and competition take the place of eager anticipation and shared delight in learning. Although we may find out by such

methods whether children have learned (at least temporarily) certain closely specified facts and skills, we do not get a full picture of what each unique child has learned and how he or she has built on the gifts we offer. What we learn in the daily reciprocity of caring goes far deeper than test results.[22]

Caring and love, so absent in educational discourse, serve to remind us that schools are inhabited by people, not sets of test scores. Schools are not the numbers they produce, they are the people who make up a living community that will flourish only when healthy. This requires love, caring, and, to echo Rowling, a passion for "imagining better." We must strive to act on the idea that such things truly matter; if we are at all lucky and smart, it will serve us as well as it served Harry.

Notes

Introduction: Why Harry?

1. J. K. Rowling, *Harry Potter and the Sorcerer's Stone* (New York: Scholastic, 1997), 17. (Said by Minerva McGonagall to Albus Dumbledore.)
2. BBC News, "Harry Potter Finale Sales Hit 11m," *BBC News,* July 23, 2007; Motoko Rich, "Record First-Day Sales for Last 'Harry Potter' Book," *New York Times,* July 22, 2007.
3. Ben Fritz, "Box Office, Harry Potter Hits New Heights, Russell Crowe Flops," *Los Angeles Times,* November 21, 2010, http://latimesblogs.latimes.com/entertainmentnewsbuzz/2010/11/box-office-harry-potter-hits-new-heights-russell-crowe-flops.html.
4. See, for example, Susan Gunelius, *Harry Potter: The Story of a Global Business Phenomenon* (New York: Palgrave Macmillan, 2008).
5. http://www.jkrowling.com/.
6. Shayna Garlick, "Harry Potter and the Magic of Reading," *Christian Science Monitor,* May 2, 2007, http://www.csmonitor.com/2007/0502/p13s01-legn.html.
7. Yankelovich and Scholastic, *2008 Kids & Family Reading Report: Reading in the 21st Century: Turning the Page with Technology* (New York: Scholastic, 2008). It is important to note the potential for bias in research commissioned by the publisher of the book; we provide these statistics not as definitive proof of the series' impact, but one piece of evidence of the value of the Potter books.
8. Harrison Group and Scholastic, *2010 Kids & Family Reading Report: Turning the Page in the Digital Age* (New York: Scholastic, 2010).
9. Edmund Kern, *The Wisdom of Harry Potter: What Our Favorite Hero Teaches Us about Moral Choices* (New York: Prometheus Books, 2003), 14.
10. Gloria Ladson-Billings, *The Dreamkeepers: Successful Teachers of African American Children,* 2nd ed. (San Francisco: Jossey-Bass, 2009). Ladson-Billings describes her approach in *The Dreamkeepers* as "methodologically 'messy'" (xvii) in that her discussion focuses on both the classroom and school levels.

11. Ibid., xvi.
12. Jeffrey M. R. Duncan-Andrade and Ernest Morrell. *The Art of Critical Pedagogy: Possibilities for Moving from Theory to Practice in Urban Schools* (New York: Peter Lang, 2008), 48.
13. Carmen Luke and Allan Luke, "School Knowledge as Simulation: Curriculum in Postmodern Conditions," *Discourse: Studies in the Cultural Politics of Education* 10, no. 2 (1990); Douglas Kellner and Jeff Share, "Toward Critical Media Literacy: Core Concepts, Debates, Organizations, and Policy," *Discourse: Studies in the Cultural Politics of Education* 26, no. 3 (2005); David Buckingham, *Media Education: Literacy, Learning, and Contemporary Culture* (London: Polity, 2003).
14. Louise M. Rosenblatt, *The Reader, the Text, the Poem: The Transactional Theory of the Literary Work* (Carbondale, IL: Southern Illinois University Press, 1978); Janice Radway, *Reading the Romance: Women, Patriarchy and Popular Literature* (Chapel Hill: University of North Carolina Press, 1991); Stuart Hall, "Encoding/Decoding," in *Culture, Media, Language: Working Papers in Cultural Studies, 1972-1979*, edited by Stuart Hall et al. (London: Routledge, 1980).
15. Angela McRobbie, *Feminism and Youth Culture: From "Jackie" to "Just Seventeen"* (Boston: Unwin Hyman, 1991); Stuart Hall and Tony Jefferson, eds., *Resistance through Rituals: Youth Subcultures in Post-War Britian* (London: Routledge, 1976).
16. Marilyn Cochran-Smith and Susan L. Lytle, *Inside/Outside: Teacher Research and Knowledge* (New York: Teachers College Press, 1993), 10.
17. Marilyn Cochran-Smith and Susan L. Lytle, *Inquiry as Stance: Practitioner Research for the Next Generation* (New York: Teachers College Press, 2009), 2.
18. http://www.thehpalliance.org.
19. J. K. Rowling, Harvard University Commencement Speech, June 2008.
20. http://www.jkrowling.com/.
21. http://www.thehpalliance.org/.
22. J. K. Rowling, Harvard Speech.
23. Henry A. Giroux, "Dumbing Down Teachers: Attacking Colleges of Education in the Name of Reform (Part I)," *Truthout,* entry posted on May 25, 2010, http://www.truth-out.org/dumbing-down-teachers-attacking -colleges-educationname-reform598202010
24. Angela Montefinise, "Harry Potter: The Boy Who Lives On," *Huffington Post*, August 9, 2010, http://www.huffingtonpost.com/the-new-york-public -library/the-boy-who-lives-on_b_673380.html (Accessed August 2010).
25. Mike Newell, *Harry Potter and the Goblet of Fire* (USA/UK: Warner Bros., 2005).

1 Defending the (Not Really) Dark Arts: Teaching to Break the DADA Curse

1. J. K. Rowling, *Harry Potter and the Prisoner of Azkaban* (New York: Scholastic, 1999), 139–140.
2. Linda Darling-Hammond, *The Flat World and Education: How America's Commitment to Equity Will Determine our Future* (New York: Teachers College Press, 2010), 40.
3. J. K Rowling, *Harry Potter and the Half Blood Prince* (New York: Scholastic, 2005), 167. (This remark was made by Harry to Ron and Hermione.)
4. Diane Ravitch, *The Death and Life of the Great American School System: How Testing and Choice Are Undermining Education* (New York: Basic Books, 2010), 218–219.
5. Henry Giroux, "In Defense of Public School Teachers in a Time of Crisis," *Truthout*, entry posted on April 14, 2010, http://www.truth-out.org/in-defense-public-school-teachers-a-time-crisis58567 (Accessed May 2010).
6. Marilyn Cochran-Smith and Susan L. Lytle, *Inquiry as Stance: Practitioner Research for the Next Generation* (New York: Teacher's College Press, 2009), 9–10.
7. Darling-Hammond, *The Flat World*.
8. Ibid.
9. Ibid., 318.
10. Jonathan Kozol, *Shame of the Nation: The Restoration of Apartheid Schooling in America* (New York: Crown, 2005).
11. Lana A. Whited with M. Katherine Grimes, "What Would Harry Do? J.K. Rowling and Lawrence Kohlberg's Theories of Moral Development," in *The Ivory Tower and Harry Potter: Perspectives on a Literary Phenomenon*, edited by Lana A. Whited (Missouri: University of Missouri Press, 2004), 203.
12. Rowling, *Azkaban*, 132.
13. Ravitch, *Death and Life*, 159.
14. J. K. Rowling, *Harry Potter and the Order of the Phoenix* (New York: Scholastic, 2003), 339.
15. Robert J. Helfenbein, "Conjuring Curriculum, Conjuring Control: A Reading of Resistance in *Harry Potter and the Order of the Phoenix*," *Curriculum Inquiry* 38, no. 4 (2008), 509.
16. Rowling, *Phoenix*, 326.
17. Jim Garrison, *Dewey and Eros: Wisdom and Desire in the Art of Teaching* (New York: Teachers College Press, 1997), 122.
18. Gloria Ladson-Billings, *The Dreamkeepers: Successful Teachers of African American Children*, 2nd ed. (San Francisco: Jossey-Bass, 2009), 14.

19. Ken Futernick, *Incompetent Teachers or Dysfunctional Systems? Re-framing the Debate on Teacher Quality and Accountability* (California: West Ed, January 2010), 10.

20. Paulo Freire, *Pedagogy of the Oppressed* (New York: Continuum, 1970), 66.

21. Ibid.

22. Henry A. Giroux, "Dumbing Down Teachers: Attacking Colleges of Education in the Name of Reform (Part I)," *Truthout,* entry posted on May 25, 2010, http://www.truth-out.org/dumbing-down-teachers-attacking -colleges-education-name-reform598202010.

23. Gloria Ladson-Billings, *The Dreamkeepers*, 28–29.

24. Ibid.

25. Luis C. Moll, "Bilingual Classroom Studies and Community Analysis: Some Recent Trends," *Educational Researcher* 21 (1992): 20–24.

26. Darling-Hammond, *The Flat World*.

27. Ravitch, *Death and Life*, 194.

28. ED.gov, "New No Child Left Behind Flexibility: Highly Qualified Teachers," March 2004, http://www2.ed.gov/nclb/methods/teachers/hqtflexibility.html (Accessed August 2010).

29. Darling-Hammond, *The Flat World*, 313.

30. ED.gov, "Beyond the Bubble Tests: The Next Generation of Assessments – Secretary Arne Duncan's Remarks to State Leaders at Achieve's American Diploma Project Leadership Team Meeting," September 2, 2010, http://www .ed.gov/news/speeches/beyond-bubble-tests-next-generation-assessments -secretary-arne-duncans-remarks-state-l (Accessed September 2010).

31. Joan L. Herman, Richard S. Brown, and Eva L. Baker, "Student Assessment and Student Achievement in the California Public School System," CSE Technical Report 519 (CRESST/University of California, Los Angeles, April 2000).

32. Darling-Hammond, *The Flat World*, 259.

33. Ibid.

34. Rowling, *Azkaban*, 333.

2   Harry on the Border between Two Worlds: Reading Harry *en Español* in a Mexican American Border Community

1. Guadalupe San Miguel, *Let All of Them Take Heed: Mexican Americans and the Campaign for Education Equality in Texas, 1910–1981* (Texas: A&M University Press, 1987).

2. Anonymous teacher, 2006.
3. Miriam Jordan, "Arizona Grades Teachers on Fluency," *Wall St Journal,* April 30, 2010, http://online.wsj.com/article/SB10001424052748703572504575 213883276427528.html?mod=WSJ_hpp_MIDDLENexttoWhatsNewsTop (Accessed September 2010).
4. This community served as the research site for my doctoral work and I am a graduate of the school system.—C. Belcher
5. J. K. Rowling, *Harry Potter and the Goblet of Fire* (New York: Scholastic, 2000).
6. J. K. Rowling, *Harry Potter and the Chamber of Secrets* (New York: Scholastic, 1999).
7. Gabriel Garcia Marquez, *One Hundred Years of Solitude* (New York: Harper Perennial Modern Classics Ed., 2006).
8. Rudolfo Anaya, *Bless Me, Ultima* (New York: Warner Books, Inc., 1972).
9. Ramon Saldivar, *Chicano Narrative: The Dialectics of Difference* (Madison: The University of Wisconsin Press, 1990).
10. J. K. Rowling, *Harry Potter and the Sorcerer's Stone* (New York: Scholastic, 1997).
11. Pedro Noguera, *The Trouble with Black Boys and other Reflections on Race, Equity, and the Future of Public Education* (San Francisco: Jossey-Bass, 2008), 76–82.
12. Angela Valenzuela, *Subtractive Schooling: U.S. Mexican Youth and the Politics of Caring* (New York: SUNY Press, 1999).
13. Tamara Lucas, Rosemary Henze, and Ruben Donato, "Promoting the Success of Latino Language-Minority Students: An Exploratory Study of Six High Schools," *Harvard Educational Review* 60, no. 3 (1990): 315–340.
14. Lisa Delpit, "No Kinda Sense" in *The Skin That We Speak: Thoughts on Language and Culture in the Classroom,* edited by Lisa Delpit (New York: The New Press, 2002), 40.
15. Ibid.
16. Valenzuela, *Subtractive Schooling,* 23.
17. Gloria Ladson-Billings, *The Dreamkeepers: Successful Teachers of African American Children,* 2nd ed. (San Francisco: Jossey-Bass, 2009).
18. Ladson-Billings, *The Dreamkeepers,* 28.
19. Linda Darling-Hammond, *The Flat World and Education: How America's Commitment to Equity Will Determine Our Future* (New York: Teachers College Press, 2010), 68.
20. Mike Rose, *Possible Lives: The Promise of Public Education in America* (New York: Penguin Books, 1995).
21. Catherine Belcher, *Bordering on Success: A Portrait of the Calexico Unified School District Since Bilingual Education, 1963–2000* (Ph.D. diss., University of Pennsylvania, 2006).

22. Angela Montefinise, "Harry Potter: The Boy Who Lives On," *Huffington Post*, August 9, 2010, http://www.huffingtonpost.com/the-new-york-public-library/the-boy-who-lives-on_b_673380.html (Accessed August 2010).

23. Ibid.

24. Ibid.

25. Rick Riordan, *The Lightning Thief* (New York: Hyperion, 2005).

26. Jeff Kinney, *Diary of a Wimpy Kid: A Novel in Cartoons* (New York: Amulet Books, 2007).

3   Harry in the Classroom: Waking Sleeping Dragons

1. J. K. Rowling, *Harry Potter and the Order of the Phoenix* (New York: Scholastic, 2003), 244.

2. David Yates, *Harry Potter and the Order of the Phoenix* (USA/UK: Warner Bros., 2005).

3. Ibid.

4. David Tyack, *The One Best System: A History of Urban American Education* (Cambridge, MA: Harvard University Press, 1974).

5. Milton Chen, *Education Nation* (San Francisco: Jossey-Bass, 2010), Kindle edition, chapter 1.

6. Ibid.

7. Antonia Darder, *Culture and Power in the Classroom: A Critical Foundation for Bicultural Education* (Westport, CT: Bergin and Garvey, 1991).

8. Giselle Liza Anatol, "The Fallen Empire: Exploring Ethnic Otherness in the World of Harry Potter," in *Reading Harry Potter: Critical Essays*, edited by Giselle Liza Anatol (Westport, CT: Praeger, 2003), 165.

9. Ibid., 173.

10. Ernie Bond and Nancy Michelson, "Writing Harry's World: Children Coauthoring Hogwarts," in *Harry Potter's World: Multidisciplinary Critical Perspectives*, edited by Elizabeth E. Heilman (New York: Routledge/Falmer, 2003), 109.

11. Luis C. Moll, "Bilingual Classroom Studies and Community Analysis: Some Recent Trends," *Educational Researcher* 21 (1992): 20–24.

12. Patrick Lee, "Pottermania Lives on in College Classrooms," *CNN.com* (2008).

13. Edmund Kern, *The Wisdom of Harry Potter: What Our Favorite Hero Teaches Us about Moral Choices* (New York: Prometheus Books, 2003), 14.

14. For discussions of Potter's literary roots, see essays in collections such as Giselle Liza Anatol, *Reading Harry Potter: Critical Essays* (Westport, CT:

Praeger, 2003); Giselle Liza Anatol, *Reading Harry Potter Again: New Critical Essays* (Westport, CT: Praeger, 2009); John Granger, *Harry Potter's Bookshelf: The Great Books Behind the Hogwarts Adventures* (New York: Berkeley Books, 2009); Elizabeth E. Heilman, *Harry Potter's World: Multidisciplinary Critical Perspectives* (New York: Routledge/Falmer, 2003); and Lana A. Whited, *The Ivory Tower and Harry Potter: Perspectives on a Literary Phenomenon* (Columbia, MO: University of Missouri Press, 2004).

15. Veronica L. Schanoes, "Cruel Heroes and Treacherous Texts: Educating the Reader in Moral Complexity and Critical Reading in J.K. Rowling's Harry Potter Books," in *Reading Harry Potter: Critical Essays*, edited by Giselle Liza Anatol (Westport, CT: Praeger, 2003).

4   *Harry Potter* and the Advanced Placement (AP) Curriculum: Teaching AP English in an Urban Charter High School

1. Lana A. Whited, "Harry Potter: From Craze to Classic?" in *The Ivory Tower and Harry Potter: Perspectives on a Literary Phenomenon*, edited by Lana A. Whited (Missouri: University of Missouri Press, 2004), 9.

2. Linda Darling-Hammond, *The Flat World and Education: How America's Commitment to Equity Will Determine our Future* (New York: Teachers College Press, 2010), 43.

3. Cindy Lou Daniels, "Literary Theory and Young Adult Literature: The Open Frontier in Critical Studies," *The ALAN Review* (2006).

4. Jeffrey M. R. Duncan-Andrade and Ernest Morrell, *The Art of Critical Pedagogy: Possibilities for Moving from Theory to Practice in Urban Schools* (New York: Peter Lang, 2008), 50.

5. Gloria Ladson-Billings, *The Dreamkeepers: Successful Teachers of African American Children,* 2nd ed. (San Francisco: Jossey-Bass, 2009), x–xi.

6. Ibid.

7. Ibid.

8. Darling-Hammond, *The Flat World*.

9. Peter McLaren, "Critical Pedagogy: A Look at the Major Concepts," in *The Critical Pedagogy Reader,* 2nd ed., edited by Antonia Darder, Marta P. Baltodano, and Rodolfo Torres (New York: Routledge, 2009), 75–6.

10. Michael W. Apple, *Cultural Politics and Education* (New York: Teachers College Press, 1996), 95.

11. Lisa Delpit, "No Kinda Sense," in *The Skin That We Speak: Thoughts on Language and Culture in the Classroom,* edited by Lisa Delpit (New York: The New Press, 2002).

12. Duncan-Andrade and Morrell, *The Art of Critical Pedagogy,* 63.

13. Mark Pike, *Teaching Secondary English* (Thousand Oaks, CA: Sage, 2003).

14. Cindy Lou Daniels, "Literary Theory," 79.

15. Consider the current debate in Texas regarding social studies textbooks: http://www.dallasnews.com/sharedcontent/dws/dn/latestnews/stories/DN -sboe_13tex.ART.State.Edition1.4bfeae3.html.

16. David Tyack and Larry Cuban. *Tinkering Toward Utopia: A Century of Public School Reform* (Cambridge, MA: Harvard University Press, 1995).

17. Suzanne Collins, *The Hunger Games* (New York: Scholastic, 2008).

18. David L. Wallace and Tison Pugh, "Playing with Critical Theory in J. K. Rowling's *Harry Potter* Series," *English Journal (High School ed.)* 96, no. 3 (January 2007).

19. Heather Lattimer, *Thinking Through Genre: Units of Study in Reading and Writing Workshops Grades 4-12* (Portland, ME: Stenhouse Publishers, 2003).

5   Old Magic, New Technologies

1. J. K. Rowling, *Harry Potter and the Chamber of Secrets* (New York: Scholastic, 1999), 39.

2. Margaret J. Oakes, "Flying Cars, Floo Powder, and Flaming Torches: The Hi-Tech, Low-Tech World of Wizardry," in *Reading Harry Potter: Critical Essays, Contributions to the Study of Popular Culture,* edited by Gizelle Liza Anatol (Westport, CT: Praeger, 2003), 117–18.

3. Raymond Williams, *Keywords: A Vocabulary of Culture and Society,* Revised ed. (New York: Oxford University Press, 1976/1983), 351.

4. Peter Applebaum, "Harry Potter's World: Magic, Technoculture, and Becoming Human," in *Harry Potter's World: Multidisciplinary Critical Perspectives,* edited by Elizabeth E. Heilman (New York: Routledge/Falmer, 2002), 44.

5. For more on schools' roles in perpetuating inequalities in participation, see, for example, Ellen Seiter, *The Internet Playground* (New York: Peter Lang, 2005); Robert Samuels, "Auto-Modernity after Postmodernism: Autonomy and Automation in Culture, Technology, and Education," in *Digital Youth, Innovation, and the Unexpected,* edited by Tara McPherson (Cambridge, MA: MIT Press, 2008); and Henry Jenkins, Katie Clinton, Ravi Purushotma, Alice J. Robinson, and Margaret Weigel, "Confronting the Challenges of Participatory Culture: Media Education for the 21st Century," in *The John D. and Catherine T. MacArthur Foundation Reports on Digital Media and Learning* (Cambridge, MA: MIT Press, 2006).

6. Maggie Jones et al., "Wiring the Classroom," *New York Times Magazine*, September 19, 2010, 62.

7. Larry Cuban, *Oversold and Underused: Computers in the Classroom* (Cambridge, MA: Harvard University Press, 2001), Kindle Edition, chapter 1.

8. Lucinda Gray, Nina Thomas, and Laurie Lewis, *Educational Technology in U.S. Public Schools: Fall 2008 (NCES 2010-034)*, edited by U.S. Department of Education and National Center for Education Statistics (Washington, DC: U.S. Government Printing Office, 2010).

9. Mizuko Ito, Sonja Baumer, Matteo Bittanti, danah boyd, Rachel Cody, Becky Herr-Stephenson, et al., *Hanging Out, Messing Around, Geeking Out: Living and Learning with New Media* (Cambridge, MA: MIT Press, 2009).

10. For an overview of recent efforts and ideas about incorporating technology into classrooms, see Jessica K. Parker, *Teaching Tech-Savvy Kids: Bringing Digital Media into the Classroom, Grades 5–12* (Thousand Oaks, CA: Corwin Press, 2010).

11. PBS and Grunwald Associates, *Digitally Inclined: Teachers Increasingly Value Media and Technology* (Arlington, VA: Grunwald Associates, 2009); Brigid Barron et al., *Digital Age Teacher Preparation Council Background Paper* (New York: The Joan Ganz Cooney Center at Sesame Workshop, 2010).

12. J. K. Rowling, *Harry Potter and the Sorcerer's Stone* (New York: Scholastic, 1997), 59.

13. It is interesting to consider this detail in terms of gender and power. Although Hagrid is literally a (half) giant, and is described with primarily masculine features (e.g., his beard, his deep voice), he carries a feminine accessory that allows him to perform limited magic. This symbol of his weakness and insufficiency as a wizard parallels his limited agency and respect as a teacher and speaks to a similar marginalization of teaching because of its characterization as "women's work."

14. President's Council of Advisors on Science and Technology, *Prepare and Inspire: K-12 Education in Science, Technology, Engineering, and Math (STEM) for America's Future* (Washington, DC: Executive Office of the President, 2010).

15. Ibid., v.

16. Ibid.

17. Bernie Triling and Charles Fadel, *21st Century Skills: Learning for Life in Our Times* (San Francisco: Jossey-Bass, 2009), 7–8.

18. Esther Wojcicki and Michael Levine, "Teaching for a Shared Future: American Educators Need to Think Globally," *The Huffington Post* (2010), http://www.huffingtonpost.com/esther-wojcicki/teaching-for-a-shared-fut_b_706504.html (Accessed September 2010).

19. Courtney Cazden, Bill Cope, Norman Fairclough, Jim Gee, et al., "A Pedagogy of Multiliteracies: Designing Social Futures," *Harvard Educational Review* 66,

no. 1 (1996); Colin Lankshear and Michele Knobel, *New Literacies: Everyday Practices and Classroom Learning,* 2nd ed. (Maidenhead: Open University Press, 2006); Michele Knobel and Colin Lankshear, *A New Literacies Sampler, New Literacies and Digital Epistemologies,* (New York: P. Lang, 2007).

20. Rachel Dretzin, "Digital Nation," *Frontline* (2010).

21. David Buckingham, *Beyond Technology: Children's Learning in the Age of Digital Culture* (London: Polity Press, 2007), 16.

22. Deborah Brandt, "Sponsors of Literacy," *College Composition and Communication* 49, no. 2 (1998): 166.

23. John Palfrey and Urs Gasser, *Born Digital* (New York, Basic Books, 2008).

24. J. K. Rowling, *Harry Potter and the Prisoner of Azkaban* (New York: Scholastic, 2001).

25. David R. Cole and Mary Kalantzis, "New Media, New Learning," in *Multiliteracies in Motion: Current Theory and Practice,* edited by David R. Cole and Darren Lee Pullen (New York: Routledge, 2010), 88.

26. Ibid.

6   Entering the Forbidden Forest: Teaching Fiction and Fantasy in Urban Special Education

1. A squib is "a non-magical person born to at least one magical parent." Definition and quote taken from the FAQ on J. K. Rowling's official website: http://www.jkrowling.com/textonly/en/extrastuff_view.cfm?id=19.

2. Thomas D. Snyder and Sally A. Dillow, *Digest of Education Statistics 2009* (Washington, DC: National Center for Education Statistics, 2010), http://nces.ed.gov/programs/digest/d09/.

3. Mary T. Brownell, Paul T. Sindelar, Mary Theresa Kiely, and Louis C. Danielson, et al., "Special Education Teacher Quality and Preparation: Exposing Foundations, Constructing a New Model," *Exceptional Children* 76, no. 3 (2010).

4. Pam Hunt and John McDonnell, "Inclusive Education," in *Handbook of Developmental Disabilities,* edited by Samuel L. Odom et al. (New York: Guilford Press, 2007).

5. Shawnee Y. Wakeman, Diane M. Browder, Irene Meier, and Ann McColl, et al., "The Implications of No Child Left Behind for Students with Developmental Disabilities," *Mental Retardation and Developmental Disabilities Research Reviews* 13 (2007), 144.

6. Allegra notes: "'+' meant 'I agree'; '–' meant 'I disagree'; '!' meant 'interesting'; '?' meant 'I am confused'; 'P' meant 'I made a prediction here'; and a stick

figure of a person meant that they were able to make a personal connection to the text."

7. Michael Cole and Peg Griffin, "A Socio-Historical Approach to Re-Mediation," *The Quarterly Newsletter of the Laboratory of Comparative Human Cognition* 5, no. 4 (1983).

8. Kris D. Gutierrez, P. Zitlali Morales, and Danny C. Martinez, "Re-Mediating Literacy: Culture, Difference, and Learning for Students from Nondominant Communities," *Review of Research in Education* 33 (2009), 227.

9. Ibid.

10. Vanessa J. Morris et al., "Street Lit: Flying Off Teen Bookshelves in Philadelphia Public Libraries," *Young Adult Library Services* 5, no. 1 (2006).

11. Michael Bitz, "The Comic Book Project: Forging Alternative Pathways to Literacy," *Journal of Adolescent and Adult Literacy* 47, no. 7 (2004).

12. Michael Pawuk, "Creating a Graphic Novel Collection @ Your Library," *Young Adult Library Services* 1, no. 1 (2002); Nancy Frey and Douglas Fisher, "Using Graphic Novels, Anime, and the Internet in an Urban High School," *The English Journal* 93, no. 3 (2004).

13. Sandra Hughes-Hassell and Pradnya Rodge, "The Leisure Reading Habits of Urban Adolescents," *Journal of Adolescent & Adult Literacy* 51, no. 1 (2007), 29.

14. Walter Dean Myers, *Monster* (New York: HarperCollins, 1999).

15. Sandra Cisneros, *The House on Mango Street* (New York: Vintage, 1984/1991).

16. Angela Johnson, *The First Part Last* (New York: Simon Pulse, 2004).

17. Andrew Ratner, *Street Lit: Teaching and Reading Fiction in Urban Schools*, The Practical Guide Series (New York: McGraw-Hill, 2010).

18. Ibid., xiv.

19. Lewis Roberts, "Nightmares, Idylls, Mystery, and Hope: Walk Two Moons and the Artifice of Realism in Children's Fiction," *Children's Literature in Education* 39 (2008), 123.

20. David Elkind, *The Hurried Child: Growing up Too Fast Too Soon*, 3rd ed. (Cambridge, MA: Perseus Pub., 2001).

21. Roberts, "Nightmares, Idylls, Mystery, and Hope: Walk Two Moons and the Artifice of Realism in Children's Fiction."

22. Gerard Jones, *Killing Monsters: Why Children Need Fantasy, Super Heroes, and Make-Believe Violence* (New York: Basic Books, 2002), 11.

23. Alison Lurie, *Don't Tell the Grown-Ups: The Subversive Power of Children's Literature* (Boston: Little, Brown and Company, 1990), 110–11.

24. R. Bernstein, "The Reality of the Fantasy in the Harry Potter Stories," *The New York Times*, November 30, 1999.

25. Hughes-Hassell and Rodge, "The Leisure Reading Habits of Urban Adolescents."

26. Jeffrey Weiss, "Harry Potter Conference in Dallas Shows Magic Is Still Working," *Dallas Morning News*, July 9, 2008, http://www.dallasnews.com/sharedcontent/dws/ent/stories/070908dnglpotter.40d6e9b.html (Accessed August 2010).

7   Imagining More

1. J. K. Rowling, Harvard Commencement Speech, 2008.
2. Bob Minzesheimer, "Harry Potter Fans Enjoy a Magical Summer," *USA Today*, June 20, 2007, http://www.usatoday.com/life/books/news/2007-06-20-potter-summer_N.htm (accessed September 2010).
3. The opposition of parents and children is part of the "digital generation" argument, by which children's social uses of media and technology to operate outside of parental control is seen as problematic. See, for example, Don Tapscott, *Growing up Digital: The Rise of the Net Generation* (New York: McGraw-Hill, 1998); Don Tapscott, *Grown up Digital: How the Net Generation Is Changing Your World* (New York: McGraw-Hill, 2009); Mizuko Ito, Sonja Baumer, Matteo Bittanti, danah boyd, Rachel Cody, Becky Herr-Stephenson, et al., *Hanging Out, Messing Around, Geeking Out: Living and Learning with New Media* (Cambridge, MA: MIT Press, 2009); John Palfrey and Urs Gasser, *Born Digital: Understanding the First Generation of Digital Natives* (New York: Basic Books, 2008).
4. John Dewey, *The Child and the Curriculum and The School and Society*, combined edition (Chicago: University of Chicago Press, 1956), 31. (Italics in original)
5. http://realwizardrock.com/harry-and-the-potters/hatp-self-titled-cd/platform-nine-and-three-quarters. See also http://harryandthepotters.com/.
6. Henry A. Giroux, "Dumbing Down Teachers: Attacking Colleges of Education in the Name of Reform (Part I)," *Truthout,* entry posted on May 25, 2010, http://www.truth-out.org/dumbing-down-teachers-attacking-colleges-educationname-reform598202010.
7. For more discussion of the development of the fandom, see Melissa Annelli, *Harry, a History: The True Story of a Boy Wizard, His Fans, and Life Inside the Harry Potter Phenomenon* (New York: Pocket Books, 2008).
8. John Fiske, *Understanding Popular Culture* (London: Routledge, 1989), 28.
9. For a history and guide to "Wrock" as well as the names and locations of current Wizard Rock bands and upcoming performances, both in the United States and internationally, see the Wizrocklopedia at http://wizrocklopedia.com/.

10. http://wizrocklopedia.com/bands/band-listings. (Please note that this website does not claim to provide a comprehensive listing of Wizard Rock bands; however, we feel it is the most complete list available.)

11. See Camille Bacon-Smith, *Enterprising Women: Television Fandom and the Creation of Popular Myth* (Philadelphia: University of Pennsylvania Press, 1991); Henry Jenkins, *Textual Poachers: Television Fans & Participatory Culture, Studies in Culture and Communication* (New York: Routledge, 1992); Karen Hellekson and Kristina Busse, eds., *Fan Fiction and Fan Communities in the Age of the Internet* (Jefferson, NC: McFarland, 2006).

12. http://realwizardrock.com/more-bands/the-whomping-willows/house-of -awesome/house-of-awesome-theme-song. See also http://www.myspace.com /thewhompingwillows for more information on The Whomping Willows.

13. Edmund Kern, *The Wisdom of Harry Potter: What Our Favorite Hero Teaches Us about Moral Choices* (New York: Prometheus Books, 2003), 19.

14. www.thehpalliance.org.

15. Dumbledore to Harry regarding The Mirror of Erised, *Sorcerer's Stone*, 265.

16. Linda Darling-Hammond, *The Flat World and Education: How America's Commitment to Equity Will Determine Our Future* (New York: Teachers College Press, 2010), 313.

17. Ibid., 313–318.

18. Ibid., 318.

19. John Dewey, *Experience and Education* (New York: Collier Books Edition, 1963), 38.

20. Jeffrey M. R. Duncan-Andrade and Ernest Morrell. *The Art of Critical Pedagogy: Possibilities for Moving from Theory to Practice in Urban Schools* (New York: Peter Lang, 2008), 11–12.

21. Lev Grossman, "Love Potions and Tragic Magic," *Time Magazine*, July 17, 2005.

22. Nel Noddings, "Caring in Education," *The Encyclopedia of Informal Education* (2005). www.infed.org/biblio/noddings_caring_in_education.htm (accessed May 2008).

References

Anatol, Giselle Liza. "The Fallen Empire: Exploring Ethnic Otherness in the World of Harry Potter." In *Reading Harry Potter: Critical Essays*, edited by Giselle Liza Anatol, 163–78. Westport, CT: Praeger, 2003.

———, ed. *Reading Harry Potter: Critical Essays*, Contributions to the Study of Popular Culture. Westport, CT: Praeger, 2003.

———, ed. *Reading Harry Potter Again: New Critical Essays*. Westport, CT: Praeger, 2009.

Anaya, Rudolfo. *Bless Me, Ultima*. New York: Warner Books, Inc., 1972.

Annelli, Melissa. *Harry, a History: The True Story of a Boy Wizard, His Fans, and Life Inside the Harry Potter Phenomenon*. New York: Pocket Books, 2008.

Apple, Michael. *Cultural Politics and Education*. New York: Teacher's College Press, 1996.

Applebaum, Peter. "Harry Potter's World: Magic, Technoculture, and Becoming Human." In *Harry Potter's World: Multidisciplinary Critical Perspectives*, edited by Elizabeth E. Heilman, 25–52. New York: Routledge/Falmer, 2002.

Bacon-Smith, Camille. *Enterprising Women: Television Fandom and the Creation of Popular Myth*. Philadelphia: University of Pennsylvania Press, 1991.

Belcher, Catherine. *Bordering on Success: A Portrait of the Calexico Unified School District Since Bilingual Education 1963–2000*. Philadelphia: University of Pennsylvania, 2006.

Bitz, Michael. "The Comic Book Project: Forging Alternative Pathways to Literacy." *Journal of Adolescent and Adult Literacy* 47, no. 7 (2004): 574–86.

Bond, Ernie and Nancy Michelson, "Writing Harry's World: Children Coauthoring Hogwarts." In *Harry Potter's World: Multidisciplinary Critical Perspectives*, edited by Elizabeth E. Heilman, 109–24. New York: Routledge/Falmer, 2003.

Brandt, Deborah. "Sponsors of Literacy." *College Composition and Communication* 49, no. 2 (1998): 165–85.

Brownell, Mary T., Paul T. Sindelar, Mary Theresa Kiely, and Louis C. Danielson. "Special Education Teacher Quality and Preparation: Exposing Foundations, Constructing a New Model." *Exceptional Children* 76, no. 3 (2010): 357–77.

Buckingham, David. *Media Education: Literacy, Learning, and Contemporary Culture*. London: Polity, 2003.

———. *Beyond Technology: Children's Learning in the Age of Digital Culture*. London: Polity, 2007.

Cazden, Courtney, Bill Cope, Norman Fairclough, Jim Gee, et al. "A Pedagogy of Multiliteracies: Designing Social Futures." *Harvard Educational Review* 66, no. 1 (1996): 60.

Chen, Milton. *Education Nation: Six Leading Edges of Innovation in Our Schools*. San Francisco: Jossey-Bass, 2010.

Cisneros, Sandra. *The House on Mango Street*. New York: Vintage, 1984/1991.

Cochran-Smith, Marilyn, and Susan L. Lytle. *Inside/Outside: Teacher Research and Knowledge*. New York: Teacher's College Press, 1993.

———. *Inquiry as Stance: Practitioner Research for the Next Generation*. New York: Teacher's College Press, 2009.

Cole, David R., and Mary Kalantzis. "New Media, New Learning." In *Multiliteracies in Motion: Current Theory and Practice*, edited by David R. Cole and Darren Lee Pullen. New York: Routledge, 2010.

Cole, Michael, and Peg Griffin. "A Socio-Historical Approach to Re-Mediation." *The Quarterly Newsletter of the Laboratory of Comparative Human Cognition* 5, no. 4 (1983): 69–74.

Collins, Suzanne. *The Hunger Games*. New York: Scholastic, 2008.

Cuban, Larry. *Oversold and Underused: Computers in the Classroom*. Cambridge, MA: Harvard University Press, 2001.

Daniels, Cindy Lou. "Literary Theory and Young Adult Literature: The Open Frontier in Critical Studies." *The ALAN Review* 33, no. 2 (2006): 78–82.

Darder, Antonia. *Culture and Power in the Classroom: A Critical Foundation for Bicultural Education*. Westport, CT: Bergin and Garvey, 1991.

Darling-Hammond, Linda. *The Flat World and Education: How America's Commitment to Equity Will Determine Our Future*. New York: Teacher's College Press, 2010.

Delpit, Lisa. "No Kinda Sense." In *The Skin That We Speak: Thoughts on Language and Culture in the Classroom*, edited by Lisa Delpit, 31–48. New York: The New Press, 2002.

Dewey, John. *The Child and the Curriculum and the School and Society, Combined Edition*. Chicago: University of Chicago Press, 1956.

Dewey, John. *Experience and Education*. New York: Collier Books Edition, 1963.

Dretzin, Rachel. "digital_nation." *Frontline*, 2010.

Duncan-Andrade, Jeffrey M. R., and Ernest Morrell. *The Art of Critical Pedagogy: Possibilities for Moving from Theory to Practice in Urban Schools*. New York: Peter Lang, 2008.

Durkheim, E. (1938/1977). *The Evolution of Educational Thought: Lectures on the Formation and Development of Secondary Education in France*. London: Routledge and Kegan Paul.

Elkind, David. *The Hurried Child: Growing Up Too Fast Too Soon*, 3rd ed. Cambridge, MA: Perseus, 2001.

Fiske, John. *Understanding Popular Culture*. London: Routledge, 1989.

Frey, Nancy, and Douglas Fisher. "Using Graphic Novels, Anime, and the Internet in an Urban High School." *The English Journal* 93, no. 3 (2004): 19–25.

Friere, Paulo. *Pedagogy of the Oppressed*. New York: Continuum, 1970.

Futernick, Ken. *Incompetent Teachers or Dysfunctional Systems? Re-Framing the Debate on Teacher Quality and Accountability*. San Francisco: WestEd, 2010.

Garlick, Shayna. "Harry Potter and the Magic of Reading," *Christian Science Monitor*, May 2, 2007, http://www.csmonitor.com/2007/0502/p13s01-legn.html.

Garrison, Jim. *Dewey and Eros: Wisdom and Desire in the Art of Teaching*. New York: Teacher's College Press, 1997.

Granger, John. *Harry Potter's Bookshelf: The Great Books Behind the Hogwarts Adventures*. New York: Berkeley Books, 2009.

Gray, Lucinda, Nina Thomas, and Laurie Lewis. *Educational Technology in U.S. Public Schools: Fall 2008 (NCES 2010-034)*, edited by U.S. Department of Education and National Center for Education Statistics. Washington, DC: U.S. Government Printing Office, 2010.

Gunelius, Susan. *Harry Potter: The Story of a Global Business Phenomenon*. New York: Palgrave Macmillan, 2008.

Gutierrez, Kris D., P. Zitlali Morales, and Danny C. Martinez. "Re-Mediating Literacy: Culture, Difference, and Learning for Students from Non-dominant Communities." *Review of Research in Education* 33 (2009): 212–45.

Hall, Stuart. "Encoding/Decoding." In *Culture, Media, Language: Working Papers in Cultural Studies, 1972–1979*, edited by Stuart Hall, Dorothy Hobson, Andrew Lowe, and Paul Willis, 107–16. London: Routledge, 1980.

Hall, Stuart, and Tony Jefferson, eds. *Resistance through Rituals: Youth Subcultures in Post-War Britain*. London: Routledge, 1976.

Harrison Group, and Scholastic. *2010 Kids & Family Reading Report: Turning the Page in the Digital Age*. New York: Scholastic, 2010.

Heilman, Elizabeth E., ed. *Harry Potter's World: Multidisciplinary Critical Perspectives*. New York: Routledge/Falmer, 2003.

Helfenbein, Robert J. "Conjuring Curriculum, Conjuring Control: A Reading of Resistance in Harry Potter and the Order of the Phoenix." *Curriculum Inquiry* 38, no. 4 (2008): 499–513.

Hellekson, Karen, and Kristina Busse, eds. *Fan Fiction and Fan Communities in the Age of the Internet*. Jefferson, NC: McFarland, 2006.

Herman, Joan L., Richard S. Brown, and Eva L. Baker. "Student Assessment and Student Achievement in the California Public School System." In *CSE Technical Report*. Los Angeles: CRESST/University of California Los Angeles, 2000.

Hughes-Hassell, Sandra, and Pradnya Rodge. "The Leisure Reading Habits of Urban Adolescents." *Journal of Adolescent & Adult Literacy* 51, no. 1 (2007): 22–33.

Hunt, Pam, and John McDonnell. "Inclusive Education." In *Handbook of Developmental Disabilities,* edited by Samuel L. Odom, Robert H. Horner, Martha E. Snell, and Jan Blacher, 269–91. New York: Guilford Press, 2007.

Ito, Mizuko, Sonja Baumer, Matteo Bittanti, danah boyd, Rachel Cody, Becky Herr-Stephenson, et al. *Hanging Out, Messing Around, Geeking Out: Living and Learning with New Media*. Cambridge, MA: MIT Press, 2009.

Jenkins, Henry. *Textual Poachers: Television Fans & Participatory Culture*, Studies in Culture and Communication. New York: Routledge, 1992.

Jenkins, Henry, Katie Clinton, Ravi Purushotma, Alice J. Robinson, and Margaret Weigel. "Confronting the Challenges of Participatory Culture: Media Education for the 21st Century." In *The John D. and Catherine T. MacArthur Foundation Reports on Digital Media and Learning*. Cambridge, MA: MIT Press, 2006.

Johnson, Angela. *The First Part Last*. New York: Simon Pulse, 2004.

Jones, Gerard. *Killing Monsters: Why Children Need Fantasy, Super Heroes, and Make-Believe Violence*. New York: Basic Books, 2002.

Kellner, Douglas, and Jeff Share. "Toward Critical Media Literacy: Core Concepts, Debates, Organizations, and Policy." *Discourse: Studies in the Cultural Politics of Education* 26, no. 3 (2005): 369–86.

Kern, Edmund. *The Wisdom of Harry Potter: What Our Favorite Hero Teaches Us About Moral Choices*. New York: Prometheus Books, 2003.

Kinney, Jeff. *Diary of a Wimpy Kid: A Novel in Cartoons*. New York: Amulet Books, 2007.

Knobel, Michele, and Colin Lankshear. *A New Literacies Sampler*, New Literacies and Digital Epistemologies. New York: Peter Lang, 2007.

Kozol, Jonathan. *Shame of the Nation: The Restoration of Apartheid Schooling in America*. New York: Crown, 2005.

Ladson-Billings, Gloria. *The Dreamkeepers: Successful Teachers of African American Children*, 2nd ed. San Francisco: Jossey-Bass, 2009.

Lankshear, Colin, and Michele Knobel. *New Literacies: Everyday Practices and Classroom Learning,* 2nd ed. Maidenhead: Open University Press, 2006.

Lattimer, Heather. *Thinking Through Genre: Units of Study in Reading and Writing Workshops Grades 4–12*. Portland: Stenhouse Publishers, 2003.

Lucas, Tamara, Rosemary Henze, and Ruben Donato. "Promoting the Success of Latino Language-minority Students: An Exploratory Study of Six High Schools." *Harvard Educational Review* 60, no. 3 (1990): 315–40.

Luke, Carmen, and Allan Luke. "School Knowledge as Simulation: Curriculum in Postmodern Conditions." *Discourse: Studies in the Cultural Politics of Education* 10, no. 2 (1990): 75–91.

Lurie, Alison. *Don't Tell the Grown-Ups: The Subversive Power of Children's Literature.* Boston: Little, Brown and Company, 1990.

Marquez, Gabriel Garcia. *One Hundred Years of Solitude.* New York: Harper Perennial Modern Classics Ed., 2006.

McLaren, Peter. "Critical Pedagogy: A Look at the Major Concepts." In *The Critical Pedagogy Reader,* 2nd ed., edited by Antonia Darder, Marta P. Baltodano, and Rodolfo Torres. New York: Routledge, 2009.

McRobbie, Angela. *Feminism and Youth Culture: From "Jackie" to "Just Seventeen".* Boston: Unwin Hyman, 1991.

Pawuk, Michael. "Creating a Graphic Novel Collection @ Your Library." *Young Adult Library Services* 1, no. 1 (2002).

Moll, Lewis C. "Bilingual Classroom Studies and Community Analysis: Some Recent Trends." *Educational Researcher* 21, no. 2 (1992): 20–4.

Morris, Vanessa J., et al., "Street Lit: Flying Off Teen Bookshelves in Philadelphia Public Libraries." *Young Adult Library Services* 5, no. 1 (2006).

Myers, Walter Dean. *Monster.* New York: HarperCollins, 1999.

Newell, Mike. *Harry Potter and the Goblet of Fire.* USA/UK: Warner Bros., 2005.

Noddings, Nel. "Caring in Education." *The Encyclopedia of Informal Education* (2005).

Noguera, Pedro. *The Trouble with Black Boys and Other Reflections on Race, Equity, and the Future of Public Education.* San Francisco: Jossey-Bass, 2008.

Oakes, Margaret J. "Flying Cars, Floo Powder, and Flaming Torches: The Hi-Tech, Low-Tech World of Wizardry." In *Reading Harry Potter: Critical Essays,* edited by Gizelle Liza Anatol, 117–30. Westport, CT: Praeger, 2003.

Palfrey, John, and Urs Gasser. *Born Digital: Understanding the First Generation of Digital Natives.* New York: Basic Books, 2008.

Parker, Jessica K. *Teaching Tech-Savvy Kids: Bringing Digital Media into the Classroom, Grades 5–12.* Thousand Oaks, CA: Corwin Press, 2010.

PBS and Grunwald Associates. *Digitally Inclined: Teachers Increasingly Value Media and Technology.* Arlington, VA: Grunwald Associates, 2009.

Pike, Mark. *Teaching Secondary English.* Thousand Oaks, CA: Sage, 2003.

President's Council of Advisors on Science and Technology. *Prepare and Inspire: K-12 Education in Science, Technology, Engineering, and Math (STEM) for America's Future.* Washington, DC: Executive Office of the President, 2010.

Radway, Janice. *Reading the Romance: Women, Patriarchy and Popular Literature.* Chapel Hill: University of North Carolina Press, 1991.

Ratner, Andrew. *Street Lit: Teaching and Reading Fiction in Urban Schools.* New York: McGraw-Hill, 2010.

Ravich, Diane. *The Death and Life of the Great American School System: How Testing and Choice Are Undermining Education.* New York: Basic Books, 2010.

Riordan, Rick. *The Lightning Thief.* New York: Hyperion, 2005.

Roberts, Lewis. "Nightmares, Idylls, Mystery, and Hope: Walk Two Moons and the Artifice of Realism in Children's Fiction." *Children's Literature in Education* 39 (2008): 121–134.

Rose, Mike. *Possible Lives: The Promise of Public Education in America.* New York: Penguin Books, 1995.

Rosenblatt, Louise M. *The Reader, the Text, the Poem: The Transactional Theory of the Literary Work.* Carbondale, IL: Southern Illinois University Press, 1978.

Rowling, J. K. *Harry Potter and the Sorcerer's Stone.* New York: Scholastic, 1998.

———. *Harry Potter and the Chamber of Secrets.* New York: Scholastic, 1999.

———. *Harry Potter and the Prisoner of Azkaban.* New York: Scholastic, 1999.

———. *Harry Potter and the Goblet of Fire.* New York: Scholastic, 2000.

———. *Harry Potter and the Order of the Phoenix.* New York: Scholastic, 2003.

———. *Harry Potter and the Half-Blood Prince.* New York: Scholastic, 2005.

———. *Harry Potter and the Deathly Hallows.* New York: Scholastic 2007.

Saldivar, Antoino. *Chicano Narratives: The Dialects of Difference.* Madison, WI: The University of Wisconsin Press, 1990.

Samuels, Robert. "Auto-Modernity after Postmodernism: Autonomy and Automation in Culture, Technology, and Education." In *Digital Youth, Innovation, and the Unexpected*, edited by Tara McPherson, 219–40. Cambridge, MA: MIT Press, 2008.

San Miguel, Guadalupe. *Let All of Them Take Heed: Mexican American and the Campaign for Educational Equality in Texas, 1910–1981.* Austin, TX: University of Texas Press, 1987.

Schanoes, Veronica L. "Cruel Heroes and Treacherous Texts: Educating the Reader in Moral Complexity and Critical Reading in J.K. Rowling's Harry Potter Books." In *Reading Harry Potter: Critical Essays*, edited by Giselle Liza Anatol. Westport, CT: Praeger, 2003.

Seiter, Ellen. *The Internet Playground.* New York: Peter Lang, 2005.

Snyder, Thomas D., and Sally A. Dillow. *Digest of Education Statistics 2009.* Washington, DC: National Center for Education Statistics, 2010.

Tapscott, Don. *Growing up Digital: The Rise of the Net Generation.* New York: McGraw-Hill, 1998.

———. *Grown up Digital: How the Net Generation Is Changing Your World.* New York: McGraw-Hill, 2009.

Trilling, Bernie, and Charles Fadel. *21st Century Skills: Learning for Life in Our Times.* San Francisco: Jossey-Bass, 2009.

Tyack, David. *The One Best System: A History of American Urban Education.* Cambridge, MA: Harvard University Press, 1974.

Tyack, David, and Larry Cuban. *Tinkering toward Utopia: A Century of Public School Reform.* Cambridge, MA: Harvard University Press, 1995.

U.S. Department of Education. Beyond the Bubble Tests: The Next Generation of Assessments – Secretary Arne Duncan's Remarks to State Leaders at Achieve's American Diploma Project Leadership Team Meeting. September 2, 2010. Retrieved October 2010 from http://www.ed.gov/news/speeches/beyond-bubble-tests-next-generation-assessments-secretary-arne-duncans-remarks-state-l.

———. *New No Child Left Behind Flexibility: Highly Qualified Teachers,* edited by Department of Education. Washington, DC: U.S. Department of Education, 2004.

Valenzuela, Angela. *Subtractive Schooling: U.S.-Mexican Youth and the Politics of Caring.* SUNY Press: Albany, NY, 1999.

Wagner, Tony. *The Global Achievement Gap: Why Even Our Best Schools Don't Teach the New Survival Skills Our Children Need–and What We Can Do About It.* New York: Basic Books, 2008.

Wakeman, Shawnee Y., Diane M. Browder, Irene Meier, and Ann McColl. "The Implications of No Child Left Behind for Students with Developmental Disabilities." *Mental Retardation and Developmental Disabilities Research Reviews* 13 (2007): 143–50.

Wallace, David L., and Tison Pugh. "Playing with Critical Theory in J.K. Rowling's Harry Potter Series." *English Journal (High School ed.)* 96, no. 3 (2007): 97–100.

Whited, Lana A. "Harry Potter: From Craze to Classic?" In *The Ivory Tower and Harry Potter: Perspective on a Literary Phenomenon,* edited by Lana A. Whited, 1–14. Columbia, MO: University of Missouri Pres, 2004.

———, ed. *The Ivory Tower and Harry Potter: Perspectives on a Literary Phenomenon.* Columbia, MO: University of Missouri Press, 2004.

Whited, Lana A., and M. Catherine Grimes. "What Would Harry Do? J.K. Rowling and Lawrence Kohlberg's Theories of Moral Development." In *The Ivory Tower and Harry Potter: Perspectives on a Literary Phenomenon,* edited by Lana A. Whited, 182–210. Columbus, MO: University of Missouri Press, 2004.

Williams, Raymond. *Keywords: A Vocabulary of Culture and Society Revised Edition.* New York: Oxford University Press, 1976/1983.

Yankelovich and Scholastic. *2008 Kids & Family Reading Report: Reading in the 21st Century: Turning the Page with Technology.* New York: Scholastic, 2008.

Yates, David. *Harry Potter and the Order of the Phoenix.* USA/UK: Warner Bros., 2005.

Index

CPSIA information can be obtained at www.ICGtesting.com
Printed in the USA
BVOW012104230512

290860BV00002B/2/P